BARRON'S DOG BIBLES

Siberian Huskies

Pam and Bob Thomas

BARRON'S

Acknowledgments

Our deepest respect and gratitude goes to our dogs, whose companionship made this book possible. Each one has influenced our understanding and made us better stewards of the breed. Special thanks to Georgia Gehrmann for her objectivity and Kay Hallberg for her perception.

About the Authors

Pam and Bob Thomas got their first Siberian in 1978. After she chewed an 18 inch hole in the wall and destroyed most of the furniture, they decided to learn a little about the breed. Since then, they've bought two houses for the dogs, 6 vehicles for the dogs (not counting rigs, sleds, and ATVs), and countless airline tickets to travel the world in search of the breed's history. Pam and Bob have participated in almost every aspect of dog sports with their Siberians, including obedience, sprint and mid-distance racing, and showing their dogs to their championships and group placings. The primary focus of their very limited breeding program was always to retain the work ethic of the breed. Iditarod, Yukon Quest and Montana 500 finishers, middle distance race winners, and competitive sprint dogs have come from their kennel. Offspring of their dogs are racing in Europe and across the U.S.

Bob's interest in the history of the Siberian Husky began innocently enough some 27 years ago. Since then, he has done research on site in Alaska, Canada, New England, and Europe and has amassed thousands of photographs, manuscripts, rare books, and artifacts pertaining to the Siberian Husky. His writings have been published in the U.S. and abroad in magazines, books, and on the web. Bob has also done consultations and interviews, television productions such as The History Channel's series, *This Week In History*, and the Japanese network, Asahi Broadcasting Corporation. He developed, and provided materials for the American Kennel Club Museum of the Dog exhibit of the Siberian Husky in 2000 and his history seminar is enjoyed by Siberian owners and prospective judges in Canada, Australia, Finland, Europe, and the U.S.

When Pam Thomas took over the editorship of the International Siberian Husky Club NEWS in 1989, Bob became a regular contributor. In the process of gathering material for the Club's 3rd Edition of *The International Siberian Husky Club, Inc. presents The Siberian Husky*, a comprehensive study of the breed edited by Pam, the Thomases met and established an enduring friendship with the family of Leonhard Seppala. Under Bob's stewardship, Seppala's previously unpublished writings, photographs, and other artifacts have been made available to Siberian fanciers in the U.S. and abroad. And the search goes on . . . with luck, they might someday be able to positively identify Molinka!

All information and advice contained in this book has been reviewed by a veterinarian.

A Word About Pronouns

Many dog lovers feel that the pronoun "it" is not appropriate when referring to a pet that can be such a wonderful part of our lives. For this reason, Siberians are described as "he" throughout this book unless the topic specifically relates to female dogs. This by no means infers any preference, nor should it be taken as an indication that either sex is particularly problematic.

Cover Credits

Dreamstime.com: front cover; Shutterstock: back cover.

Photo Credits

123rf.com: page 168; Seth Casteel: pages 59, 60, 153; Kent Dannen: page 119; Shirley Fernandez/Paulette Johnson: page 110; Jeanmfogle.com: page 129; From the collection of Sigrid Seppala Hanks: pages 5, 13; From the collection of Sigrid Seppala Hanks, Photo by H. G. Kaiser, 1911: page 6; From the collection of Sigrid Seppala Hanks, Photo by H. G. Kaiser, 1912: page 2; iStockphoto: pages 25, 30, 165; Daniel Johnson/Paulette Johnson: pages 57, 65, 78, 79, 86, 108, 140 (top and bottom), 141 (top and bottom), 142 (top and bottom), 143 (top and bottom), 144 (top and bottom), 145 (top and bottom); Shutterstock: pages i, iii, vi, 9, 10, 14, 15, 16, 18, 24, 26, 33, 34, 35, 37, 38, 39, 40, 44, 46, 51, 52, 55, 56, 67, 70, 74, 81, 90, 97, 98, 100, 103, 106, 114, 120, 123, 131, 137, 158, 162, 166, 170, 172, 173, 174, 178; Connie Summers/Paulette Johnson: pages 63, 117; Joan Hustace Walker: pages 22, 76, 85, 89, 95, 111, 112, 125, 133, 146, 148, 149, 150, 151, 153, 155, 156, 157, 160.

All inquiries should be addressed to:
Barron's Educational Series, Inc.
250 Wireless Boulevard
Hauppauge, New York 11788
www.barronseduc.com

ISBN: 978-0-7641-6379-1 (book)
ISBN: 978-0-7641-8678-3 (DVD)
ISBN: 978-1-4380-7021-6 (package)

Library of Congress Catalog Card No: 2010054132

Library of Congress Cataloging-in-Publication Data

Thomas, Pam, 1951–
    Siberian huskies / Pam and Bob Thomas.
        p. cm. — (Barron's dog bibles)
    Includes index.
    ISBN 978-0-7641-6379-1
    1. Siberian husky. I. Thomas, Bob, 1949– II. Title.
    SF429.S65T46 2011
    636.73--dc22   2010054132

Printed in China

9 8 7 6 5 4 3 2 1

CONTENTS

CONTENTS

Our first Siberian, Nettie, was a reclamation project in every sense. She came to us a foundling, frightened of her own shadow. It took a while, and we learned a lot about socialization and Siberian temperament in the intervening years, but in the end, Nettie's desire to run helped her overcome her fears.

Our first experienced lead dog came to us off an open-class sprint team. Nine-year-old Earnie the Wonderdog, sire of our first home-bred champion, had a presence that literally oozed confidence. His exploits at lead became the stuff of legend, and his ability to train younger lead dogs remains unequaled. He taught us more in one racing season than we had learned from other humans in the previous five.

We've been owned by many Siberians over the past 30 years, each with his or her own unique personality, each an individual in his or her own right. We've been humbled, embarrassed, thrilled, and, on occasion, left speechless by our dogs, and we wouldn't trade the experiences we've shared with each one of them for anything in the world. It would be an understatement to say that Siberians are different; they are in spades, and that's why we love them. We respect that the quintessential Siberian is a natural endurance runner, driven by his innate curiosity to see what's around the next bend in the trail.

And yes, he's also an intelligent escape artist, a digger, and many other things both good and bad. If you're lucky enough to have a Siberian, then you're already well aware of this, and our hope is that you'll find in this book the information you need and can use to become a better student of the breed. If you're considering adding a Siberian to your household, this book has the information you need to make the right decision, because Siberians are not the breed for everyone. They demand an owner committed to providing attention, exercise, and vigilant supervision. But if you're sure you were meant to be owned by one, this book is your guide to understanding, adapting, and living happily with the indomitable spirit that is the Siberian Husky.

Chapter One

All About Siberian Huskies

The Siberian sled dog survived for thousands of years in one of the harshest climates on earth—northeast arctic Siberia. Superbly adapted to the environment in which it evolved, the breed is a living example of the canine species in its most primitive form.

Siberian Sled Dogs

Anthropologists hypothesize that early pariah dogs originated in Asia and migrated with nomadic human groups both south to Africa and north to the Arctic. Recent studies of the canine genome have established the Siberian Husky as one of the best living representatives of this ancestral dog gene pool. It is not known exactly when the indigenous peoples of the Arctic first began using dogs to pull sleds, but archeological research indicates that dogs were present at Paleoeskimo camps between 3,000 and 4,000 years ago. Over centuries of relative isolation, sled dogs with different characteristics evolved to suit the climate, terrain, and purpose, resulting in the breeds we know today as the Samoyed and the Siberian Husky.

The people of northeast Siberia most often associated with the Siberian Husky are the Chukchi, an aboriginal arctic people traditionally divided into two subgroups. The Reindeer Chukchi lived on the inland tundra and taiga raising deer, and spent the year moving with their herds. Their dogs were used primarily as hunters and pack animals. The coastal, or Maritime, Chukchi maintained more permanent settlements along the arctic coast and, according to many researchers, were the first to seriously depend on their sled dogs for survival.

The Chukchi, effectively isolated by their environment, developed a sled dog perfectly adapted to the northern arctic desert, where food was always scarce. The Chukchi's dog, relatively small and light on his feet, could travel long distances with ease on scant snow packed hard by coastal winds, and do it on remarkably little food. A double coat, medium-sized ears, and almond-shaped eyes protected the dog from wind and relentless cold. A congenial temperament made the dogs easy to handle when the Chukchi, who often drove teams of 16 to 20 dogs, needed to get far out onto the sea ice and back quickly. In summer, the Chukchi dog was turned loose to survive on mice, rabbits, and spawning salmon that he caught himself. This dog's combination of speed, endurance, and efficiency served the Chukchi well when, in the 1600s, Russian Cossacks invaded Siberia.

By the 1700s, most indigenous Siberian tribes, including the Koryaks, Yukagirs, and Kamchadals, were fighting back but were no match for the Cossacks and their weaponry. The Chukchi, though, with their fast, efficient sled dog teams, could run from the Cossacks and were never completely subjugated by Russia. However, as a result of the Russian occupation of Siberia, the Siberian tribes no longer existed in isolation, and by the end of the eighteenth century, trade between the Chukchi, other Siberian tribes, and American whalers and fur traders was common. And so it was, under conditions existing in northeast Siberia at the time, that the first documented importation of Siberian dogs to Nome, Alaska, occurred in 1908.

East to Alaska

Nome, Alaska, in the southwest corner of the Seward Peninsula on Norton Sound, was in 1908 the largest city in the Territory of Alaska. Gold had been discovered nearby in 1898, and the city was awash in prospectors and all the commerce needed to support the gold rush. Because it was completely isolated in winter, with Norton Sound frozen and hundreds of uninhabited

miles between them and the outside world, dog teams were the transport of choice for Nomeites. There were many good dog teams in Nome made up of a mix of indigenous malamute-looking animals (not the purebred Alaskan Malamute of today) and large dogs imported from Seattle and San Francisco by gold seekers. Given the number of dog teams and the wealth that existed in Nome at the time, racing those teams against each other, and betting on the results, was inevitable.

The Nome Kennel Club was established in 1907 to promote and stage sled dog races. One of the first, and most popular, was the All Alaska Sweepstakes, a 408-mile (653 km) race from Nome to Candle and back. In 1908, 10 teams competed—the winner completing the course in 119 hours, 15 minutes, and 12 seconds. William Goosak, a Russian fur trader, saw the April 1908 Sweepstakes race and realized that the format and length of the trail would favor the Chukchi sled dogs he had seen in Siberia. In the fall of that year, Goosak brought at least 10 dogs from the Anadyr Gulf area of Siberia to Nome. The team of 10 "Siberian rats," a 40-to-1 long shot at the starting line, took third place in the 1909 All Alaska Sweepstakes, stunning local dog watchers. Although their exhausted driver, Thrustrup, collapsed at the finish line, the dogs were alert and playful, suggesting to many that a more experienced driver could have won. One such believer was Charles Fox Maule-Ramsay, a young Scottish nobleman with family mining interests in Nome. So convinced of the Siberian dog's capabilities was Ramsay that he chartered a schooner to Markovo, a trading settlement 250 miles (400 km) inland on the Anadyr River. The approximately 50 Siberians Ramsay brought to Nome were divided among three teams for the 1910 All Alaska Sweepstakes. John "Iron Man" Johnson, driving Ramsay's Team 1, won the race, setting a record that held up for 98 years. Ramsay himself placed second, and more significantly, assured the breed of a place in history.

Fun Facts

A Rose by Any Other Name

When the first imports arrived in Nome, Alaska, no one was impressed with the little dogs weighing only 40 to 52 pounds (18–23 kg). In fact, Nomeites referred to them as "Siberian rats"—Siberian because that's where they came from, and rats because they were so much smaller than other sled dogs in Nome at the time. Newspapers reporting sled dog races in both Alaska and New England through the 1920s referred to them as "Siberian dogs." The addition of *Husky* to the Siberian's name does not appear in print until 1929, just before the breed was recognized by the American Kennel Club in 1930. The word *Husky*, used in modern times to refer to any sled dog that has typically northern dog characteristics such as a thick coat and pointed, upright ears, comes from the slang word for Eskimo, *Esky*.

Leonhard Seppala, the true "founder" of the modern Siberian Husky breed, arrived in Nome in the summer of 1900 from Norway. By 1913, when famed explorer Roald Amundsen announced plans to reach the North Pole via Nome and Barrow, Seppala was the most experienced dog driver the Pioneer Mining Company had in their employ. Pioneer acquired 15 Siberian dogs from the Nome area and assigned them to Seppala for training, expecting to present the team to Amundsen when he arrived in the summer of 1914. World War I canceled Amundsen's journey, but Seppala and those Siberians would go on to dominate the All Alaska Sweepstakes from 1915 until America's entry into WWI, and the subsequent dwindling of Nome's population caused the race's demise in 1917.

Dog teams did much more than race, of course. Their primary purpose was hauling freight, passengers, and mail hundreds of miles, and making surveying trips totaling thousands of miles. There are also several well-documented accounts of dog teams asked to race against death. Esther Darling's poem, "Seppala Drives to Win!," for example, recounts how Seppala and 17 Siberians, led by Russky, tried to save the fatally injured Bobby Brown. With Brown in the sled, the team raced 58 miles (93 km) over unfamiliar territory in the dark, in minus-30-degree (–34°C) temperatures, in seven and a half hours. Famous leaders such as Russky, Kolyma, and Togo were already household names in Alaska when the events of 1925 brought them worldwide acclaim. On January 22, 1925, a six-year-old boy living in Nome died of diphtheria. Getting antitoxin to that isolated town quickly was crucial, but how? There were neither roads nor trains to Nome. The sea was frozen, and aviation, still in its infancy, was too dangerous. The only means available was also the most reliable—the sled dog team. The Serum Run of 1925, also known as the Great Race of Mercy, called for shipping serum from Anchorage to Nenana by rail, then relaying it by dog team 674 miles (1,078 km) to Nome. At the time, a single team could be expected to cover that trail in about two weeks in good weather. Two weeks was too long for diphtheria-stricken Nome, of course, and the weather was anything but good in January 1925. Most of the 674 miles (1,078 km) was run in the polar night through one of the worst storms in memory, with temperatures hovering between 20 and 64 below zero (–29 and –53.3°C) and windchills of minus 70 (–57°C). Yet each leg of the relay was played out in the headlines and on radio around the world. It took just five and a half days (127.5 hours) for the 20 dog teams to carry the first fur-wrapped package the distance.

Fun Facts

Mush

Nomeites initially referred to the men who managed sled dog teams as "dog drivers." French Canadian explorers urged their teams forward with a commanding "Ma-a-r-r-che!" which to the English-speaking settlers of the Canadian north sounded like "Mush!" Thus, dog drivers became known as "mushers," but they use commands such as "All right" or "Get up," never "Mush," to get the team going. As the frigid wilds of North America were opened to travel, the "dog-puncher" earned his living hauling the mail, passengers, and freight by dog team.

Yes, in fact, there were two relays. Gunnar Kaasen and his Siberian team arrived in Nome with the first package of serum at 5:30 A.M. on February 2, 1925. By February 8, a second relay by sled dog team carrying antitoxin had begun in Nenana. With many of the same drivers participating, the second shipment arrived in Nome on February 15, the diphtheria epidemic was stopped, and the quarantine was lifted. Aside from a certificate and the eternal gratitude of the people of Nome, accounts vary about what each driver received in compensation. Leonhard Seppala and his Siberians received most of the credit for the Serum Run because they traveled the greatest distance over the most dangerous terrain, but in the end, the serum was delivered and Nome was saved because of the endurance and courage of all the sled dogs and their drivers. For the Siberians, what happened next would ensure the breed a place in the hearts of dog mushers and fanciers for years to come.

Siberians Go Outside

Leaving Alaska to go south to the United States (Alaska was a territory until 1959) was, and still is, called going "Outside." Shortly after Nome was saved by the Serum Run, Leonhard Seppala was asked to go on a publicity tour, an exciting prospect for the gregarious Norwegian. He could showcase his dogs and, more importantly, arrive in New England in winter, where sled dog racing had become a popular winter sport. Seppala left Nome with 42 Siberians, bound for Seattle, in October 1926. He and the Siberians next visited Kansas City, then Dayton, and Providence, Rhode Island, among other places. At Madison Square Garden in New York City, in front of a packed house, the arctic explorer Roald Amundsen presented the famous Siberian lead dog, Togo, with a gold medal for his heroic role in the Serum Run.

Seppala and his Siberians got to New England in January 1927 and were soon entered at the annual Poland Spring, Maine, sled dog race. As if a replay of

Helpful Hints

Suggested Reading

The story of the Serum Run is fascinating and can be found in detail in the following:
Alaskan Trails, Siberian Dogs by John Douglas Tanner Jr.
The Cruelest Miles by Gay and Laney Salisbury
The Race to Nome by Kenneth A. Ungermann
The World of Sled Dogs by Lorna Coppinger

1908 Nome, the little Siberians were ridiculed and no one expected the calm, friendly dogs to make much of a showing. The Siberians, of course, won the race by a wide margin, and by the time the 1927 racing season was over, Seppala and his Siberians had beaten the best New England and eastern Canada had to offer. And everyone wanted dogs just like them! Seppala also wanted to keep racing in New England and Canada, so he established a kennel in Poland Spring and took back to Alaska each spring only enough dogs to get him from the train station in Nenana to Nome. Puppies and adult dogs from the Poland Spring kennel became the foundation of today's Siberian Husky, and the people who acquired these dogs were responsible for American Kennel Club recognition, which came in 1930. In a short but eventful 22-year span, the Siberian had gone from arctic village dog to recognized breed.

The Siberian was considered, in the late 1920s and early 1930s, the premier racing sled dog in a sport that was quite popular, particularly in the northeast United States and Canada, despite the Depression. Races were well covered by the press, appearing on the sports pages of newspapers such as *The New York Times* and *Boston Globe*. Media coverage increased the Siberian's visibility and popularity, drawing the attention of polar explorers and the U.S. Army. A number of Siberians were involved in the 1939 Byrd Expedition to Antarctica, including its three-month, 1,400 mile (2,240 km) surveying trek. Byrd's expedition was cut short by the start of World War II, but the U.S. Army, recognizing the unique capabilities of sled dogs, promptly drafted most of the experienced mushers and their dogs as a unit, to assist in the war effort. Almost every Siberian available at the start of the war became a U.S. Army sled dog.

Fun Facts

The Statue in Central Park

As a result of the worldwide publicity accorded the 1925 Serum Run, a bronze statue was erected in New York City's Central Park. Sculptor Frederick Roth's piece is at Fifth Avenue and 77th Street next to the Willowdell Arch and was unveiled in December 1925. The statue of a harnessed Balto has been polished to a shine by children who stroke his nose and ears, and sit on his back for photographs. The inscription reads, "Dedicated to the indomitable spirit of the sled dogs that relayed antitoxin six hundred miles over rough ice across treacherous waters through arctic blizzards from Nenana to the relief of stricken Nome in the Winter of 1925. Endurance Fidelity Intelligence."

By 1942 the army had established a sled dog training camp at Camp Rimini, Montana. Dog teams and drivers were assigned to the Air Rescue Service, and were trained to rescue downed pilots and evacuate wounded soldiers in bad weather. Ideally, two teams were landed as close as possible to a crash site and then dispatched with drivers, medics, and a radioman. At the start of the war, "as close as possible" often meant days, even weeks, of sledding to reach the crash. The need to shorten rescue time was evident, and by 1943, teams had the capability of parachuting into crash

FYI: Polar Expeditions

Siberian Huskies participated in several expeditions to the Antarctic continent, proving themselves to be the equal of any of the other breeds of sled dogs.

1939–1941—The third Byrd Expedition. Dick Moulton of Chinook Kennels took a team of Siberians to Antarctica. The highlight was a 1,400-mile (2,240-km) surveying trip, the longest distance covered by a dog team in Antarctica until 1989.

1946–1947—Operation Highjump. Led by Rear Admiral Byrd, the United States Navy Antarctic Developments Program, a.k.a. Operation Highjump, was a massive naval expedition to the Antarctic. Dog teams were employed as highly reliable rescue teams. Once again, Chinook Kennels supplied and trained the Siberian Huskies.

1955–1957—Operation Deep Freeze. This expedition was launched in support of the International Geophysical Year (a collaborative effort between 40 nations to carry out earth science studies) and led by Rear Admiral Richard Byrd. The first permanent base, initially named Naval Air Facility McMurdo, was built during this time. Once again, the Siberians served as reliable rescue teams.

sites. Colonel Norman Vaughan, a dog driver on the first Byrd Expedition and eventual commander of army sled dog operations, developed the collapsible sled and dog parachutes necessary to make jumping into crash sites safe and successful. The dogs, according to after-action reports, got excited every time they were strapped into their harnesses and wagged their tails all the way down. U.S. Army sled dogs earned their parachute wings after five jumps, the same number required for a human paratrooper. No dog was ever hurt and no sled ever damaged in a jump. At war's end, the sled dogs and their drivers were honorably discharged and credited with rescuing 150 downed fliers and evacuating 300 wounded.

The Siberian Goes Mainstream

After World War II, most Siberian fanciers in New England picked up where they had left off—mainly racing their dogs. And as more people had more disposable income in the post-war economy, sled dog racing spread to the Midwest and West, leading to the expansion of the Siberian's popularity outside New England. One thing led to another, including showing sled dogs at dog shows during the off-season, and soon, even people who lived in Florida and other places where snow is a rare commodity wanted a dog just like Pando. Between 1957 and 1961, Ch. Monadnock's Pando, a stunning black-and-white, blue-eyed male, was winning the Working Group at a time when Siberians were rarely considered. Pando's fame dramatically increased

the popularity of the Siberian across the country, and his exotic look became synonymous with the breed. Even today, those unfamiliar with the breed think the Siberian is a black-and-white dog with blue eyes.

Siberians are still active in sled dog sports, of course, but they've also become worthy competitors in conformation shows and obedience and agility trials. And if you aren't the competitive sort, your Siberian will be just as happy hiking or biking with you. The Siberian of today has come countless miles and many generations from the white wilderness of Siberia, yet this multitalented sled dog has lost none of the intelligence, athleticism, and friendliness first recognized in Nome more than a century ago.

Fun Facts

The First AKC and CKC Registrations

The first Siberian Husky to be registered by the American Kennel Club was a white female leader from Fairbanks, Alaska, named Fairbanks Princess Chena. She was born on September 16, 1927. The first Siberian to be registered by the Canadian Kennel Club after recognition in 1939 was Seppala's last famous leader, Bonzo. He was born in Alaska on July 15, 1925, and brought to Poland Spring, Maine by Seppala before being acquired by Harry Wheeler of St. Jovite, Quebec, in 1932.

Siberians in Literature

The exploits of brave AND beautiful sled dogs make great subject matter for children's books. Several such books, in fact, feature Togo and Balto of Serum Run fame in starring roles. For example, *The Bravest Dog Ever: The True Story of Balto* (Natalie Standiford) is a beginning reader's tale of Balto's role in the Serum Run; *Togo's Fireside Reflections* by Elizabeth Ricker features Togo telling his life story to the author's two children; and Robert J. Blake's *Togo* focuses on Togo and his role in the Serum Run. Debbie Miller's award-winning *The Great Serum Race: Blazing the Iditarod Trail* uses Leonhard Seppala to tell the sled dog's story.

The Siberian made his first literary appearance in the scientific journals of Russian scholar Stepan P. Krasheninnikov in 1755. Krasheninnikov, sent to explore and map Siberia for the Russian tsar Peter the Great, describes the indigenous people of Siberia and their sled dogs in detail in *Explorations of Kamchatka, 1735–1741*. Richard J. Bush, a member of the Russo-American Telegraph Expedition, published his journal of Siberian travel, *Reindeer, Dogs, and Snow-shoes*, in 1871. George Kennan's 1870 journal, *Tent Life in Siberia: Adventures Among the Koryaks and Other Tribes in Kamchatka and Northern Asia*, chronicles personal observations of native life, climate, and language during his two-year journey across Siberia as a member of the same expedition. Polar exploration and the discovery of gold fed society's fascination with the frozen north, creating even more demand for tales of the trails. Rear Admiral Richard Byrd's expeditions were chronicled by numerous members, including John O'Brien, Paul Siple, and Jack Bursey. Esther Birdsall Darling, a prolific Nome storyteller, wrote of the heroics of sled dogs named Luck, Navarre, and Boris. Several early dog drivers, including A. A. "Scotty" Allan (*Gold, Men and Dogs*), Frank Dufresne (*My Way Was North*), and Leonhard Seppala himself (*Seppala, Alaskan Dog Driver*), penned autobiographical stories of adventure and daring. Ann Mariah Cook's 1998 *Running North*, chronicles the Cook family's dream of running the Yukon Quest with their Siberian team.

Siberians in Film and TV

Who was it that said actors should never work with animals or small children? Siberians, with their good looks, expressive faces, and intelligence, are showstoppers all. Gus, the white Siberian lead dog in Disney's *Iron Will*, steals the show with behavior and facial expressions suggesting a true understanding of his circumstances. *Eight Below*, another Disney story loosely based on a 1958 Japanese scientific expedition to Antarctica, features Siberian actors hiding in snow, crawling on their bellies, opening latches, and catching fake birds suspended from high wires. One movie critic opined, "It's lucky for human actors that canines can't win Academy Awards, because, if they could, the dogs in *Eight Below* would sweep next

FYI: Mascots

Huskies are a favorite mascot for colleges and universities across North America because of their noble qualities: courage and endurance. Below are several examples of colleges and universities whose mascots are, or were, live Siberian Huskies.

Northeastern University, Boston: Sapsuk, a Siberian bred by Leonhard Seppala, became the first Northeastern Husky, in 1927. He was given an honorary degree and named King Husky forever more. After King Husky I's death in 1941, Northeastern developed a 20-year relationship with Chinook Kennels in Wonalancet, New Hampshire, which provided the next seven Siberian mascots.

University of Connecticut: UConn students chose the Husky mascot in 1934, and all but the first, a brown-and-white dog, have been pure white Siberian Huskies with one brown eye and one blue eye. The current live mascot is Jonathan XIII.

Bloomsburg University, Pennsylvania: From 1933 to 1958, a total of five dogs named Roongo represented BU's athletic prowess. Roongo is a combination of the words *maroon* and *gold*. A black-and-white, blue-eyed, costumed mascot personifies the Husky today.

University of Washington: The name *Husky* captured the true spirit of the Northwest because Seattle was recognized as the "Gateway to the Alaskan Frontier." Between 1922 and 1958, UW used Siberian Huskies as mascots, but the dogs appeared only at home games because of travel costs. A costumed student performer, Harry the Husky, was hired in 1995 to appear as a secondary mascot when the live mascot is unable to attend.

Houston Baptist University: The Huskies mascot was adopted in 1965. Samoyeds and Alaskan Malamutes were used until 1999, when the university got Wakiza, a black-and-white, blue-eyed Siberian Husky. After Wakiza's death in 2010, HBU adopted Kiza II, a gray and white, from a Siberian rescue organization.

St. Mary's University, Halifax, Nova Scotia: The Siberian Husky became the official mascot, in 1960, for qualities that paralleled the teams' motto, In Pursuit of Excellence. "Pound for pound, the Siberian Husky is the strongest draft dog in existence. A versatile and gentle dog, the Husky is the perfect example of tenacity, drive, and loyalty," says the school's calendar. A costumed mascot makes public appearances.

year's Oscars." Cuba Gooding Jr. doesn't stand a chance working opposite Diesel, Duchess, Demon, and the rest of the *Snow Dogs*, since their sole purpose as stars in the movie is to get the best of their new dog-hating owner. The actual star of *Snow Buddies* is—you guessed it!—a black-and-white, blue-eyed talking Siberian Husky puppy named Shasta.

The television show *Due South*, airing from 1994 to 1996, followed the adventures of the fictional Constable Benton Fraser, a Royal Canadian Mounted Police officer, and his sidekick, a deaf "wolf-dog" mix named Diefenbaker who could read lips in both English and Inuktitut. Dief supposedly lost his hearing fishing Fraser out of Prince Rupert Sound, but whether Diefenbaker was actually deaf, and not just suffering from selective hearing—a typically Siberian ailment—was left to the viewer to decide.

Diefenbaker was played by, naturally, purebred Siberians named Cinder, who did most of the stunts, Lincoln, and Draco.

Ten Famous Siberians

All Siberians are famous for something, be it digging the deepest hole in the neighborhood or shedding the most hair. A few, though, have achieved such fame that their names are instantly recognized by Siberian fanciers worldwide.

1. **Kolyma:** A Siberian imported to Alaska, Kolyma led the 1910 record-setting All Alaska Sweepstakes team. He also led teams in the 1911 through 1914 Sweeps, winning in 1914 when he was more than 10 years old. In 1915, Kolyma and his 1914 All Alaska Sweepstakes teammates were featured at the Panama Pacific Exposition in San Francisco.

2. **Togo:** Undoubtedly the most famous Siberian of all, Togo was Leonhard Seppala's main leader from 1918 through 1926. (See page 5 for a photo of Seppala and Togo.) Among his more well-known journeys was a 2,000-plus-mile (3,200 km) Alaska Railroad surveying trip in 1921 and the Serum Run relay in 1925. Togo was Sepp's

favorite dog, and after he died in 1929, Seppala donated Togo to Yale University for display. Togo's mount now stands in a glass case at the Iditarod Trail Sled Dog Race headquarters in Wasilla, Alaska.

3. **Balto:** Balto was credited with leading the team that delivered the diphtheria antitoxin to Dr. Welch in Nome. After the Serum Run, Balto, his driver, and the rest of the team went to Hollywood to star in the movie *Winds of Chance*. He and some of his teammates were rescued from a California exhibit by the schoolchildren of Cleveland and lived out their lives at the Cleveland Zoo. After his death in 1933, Balto was donated to the Cleveland Museum of Natural History. His mount is periodically displayed, particularly around the time of the annual Iditarod sled dog race, which commemorates the Serum Run.

4. **Fritz:** Fritz was one of Seppala's main leaders in the Serum Run, and raced in the last two All Alaska Sweepstakes races. He was Togo's half brother and co-led Sepp's teams through 1928. He died in 1932 while on display in a Christmas window at the Gimbel Brothers Department store in New York City, the last Sweepstakes dog to pass on. Fritz's mount is now at the Carrie M. McLain Memorial Museum in Nome.

5. **Bonzo:** Ch. Bonzo of Anadyr, CD, became, in 1955, the first Siberian to win an all-breed Best in Show. More importantly, Bonzo was an outstanding single leader in Alaska, placing in many of the largest races in that state.

6. **Pando:** Ch. Monadnock's Pando, the black-and-white, blue-eyed dog whose looks became synonymous with "Siberian Husky," won five consecutive Best of Breeds at Westminster and many Specialty shows. Pando and his look-alike son, Ch. Monadnock's King, won Best-Brace-in-Show repeatedly, and Pando and three of his sons often won Best-Team-in-Show.

7. **Cinnar:** In 1980, Am/Can Ch. Innisfree's Sierra Cinnar, Multiple Best in Show and Multiple Best in Specialty Show winner, became the first (and to date, the only) Siberian Husky to win Best in Show at the prestigious Westminster Kennel Club show in Madison Square Garden, in New York City. Cinnar is considered the breed's top producer of all time.

8. **Storm King:** In 1980, OTCH Storm King of Siberia became the first Siberian Husky to complete the requirements for the Obedience Trial Champion (OTCH) title. He was ranked the number one Siberian Husky in competitive obedience several times, and competed in three Super Dog obedience competitions.

9. **Monte:** In 1995, Ch. Stormwatch's Montana became the first AKC Champion Siberian Husky to finish an Iditarod Trail Sled Dog Race (1,100 miles/1,760 km). During his racing career, Monte also completed the Yukon Quest, the other 1,000-plus-mile (1,600 km) race. In 1998, Monte won Best of Opposite Sex at the Siberian Husky Club of America National Specialty.

10. **Yakut:** Alaskan's Yakut of Anadyr II led a purebred Siberian Husky Iditarod team from Anchorage to Nome in 1995, and then crossed the Bering Strait three weeks later to lead that same team to a fourth-place finish in the 1995 International HOPE race, a total of 2,000 (3,200) racing miles in just over a month. Yakut won an Award of Merit at the 1995 National Specialty from the Sled Bitch class, won Best of Breed from the Sled Bitch class at the Anchorage Specialty, and won Best Sled Dog at the 1998 National Specialty.

Chapter Two

The Mind of the Siberian Husky

Some describe the Siberian as an enigma: sometimes loving and sometimes aloof; dignified yet a goofball; happy-go-lucky but hardworking. But once you understand why the Siberian Husky exists in the first place, you can begin to understand why this strikingly beautiful and intelligent dog acts the way he does and needs the things he needs. Although the Siberian might seem a bit perplexing at times, you can be certain he'll be a friendly, outgoing, fanatic runner.

Once a Sled Dog, Always a Sled Dog

Bred exclusively to work until just several decades ago, the Siberian of today has retained all the innate behaviors that allowed his ancestors to not only survive but thrive in arctic Siberia. Ever the athlete, your Siberian spends his ideal day expending energy. While working in harness is his forte, he's quite adaptable and gregarious. He'll enjoy a long, quiet walk or an exciting day exploring with the family. But ask him to do something he dislikes, and you're likely to meet up with the Siberian's indomitable spirit, that tough intellect developed to survive the inhospitable conditions of his native Siberia.

Some breeds live to serve mankind, but the Siberian is a rugged individualist. If he finds your suggestion appealing, he'll first have to check his day planner—his is a hectic schedule of running and digging and ambushing. In his mind, your Siberian believes he can fend for himself, and he will never pass up the opportunity to do so. He doesn't need you to pamper him or fawn over him, because he will certainly not fawn over you. You're the lead dog.

He's a graceful, exuberant partner. He's also an ingenious, nomadic challenge. In one guise or another, the Siberian will always be a sled dog, doing what he was bred to do. The sled dog will always

- Be mentally tough. The Siberian's ancestors stoically survived and persevered in some of the harshest conditions on earth. They worked relentlessly in winter and had to feed themselves in summer. So, if your Siberian doesn't want to do something, a few harsh words from you will not likely change his mind.

- Be resourceful. The uninformed often deem the Siberian "too smart for his own good," when what they are actually seeing are well-developed survival instincts that allow him to find a trail in a blizzard and figure out how to operate a dog-proof latch.
- Be self-sufficient. He keeps himself meticulously clean, the better to keep his coat functioning properly. His ancestors fended for themselves in Siberia, and your Siberian, if given the opportunity, will do the same with efficiency, speed, and cunning. Vigilance is synonymous with Siberian ownership.
- Be gregarious. The Siberian's original pack was a nomadic community. People came and went with regularity, and community survival depended on friendly cooperation and shared responsibility. Your Siberian's pack, of course, could include the burglar, because, after all, the burglar is a potential friend and coworker.

Breed Truths

Siberian Personality
- Independent
- Intelligent
- Stoic
- Tenacious
- Energetic
- Alert
- Gregarious
- Nonaggressive

- Be adventuresome. The Chukchi dog was originally bred to run for long distances over a vast area. This means your Siberian will avail himself of every opportunity to stretch his legs, just to see what's around the next corner, and the next, and the next. No amount of chasing and pleading will persuade him to cancel his trip.

Yes, the Siberian is emphatically his own dog, because in his mind, he has to be; he's a sled dog. He's also a mischievous prankster with a zest for life and a seemingly endless desire to play that lasts through adulthood. Wonder where all his toys are? Look under the couch cushions. Ask him why he dug another canyon in the yard and you're likely to get a two-minute speech about the need for eco-friendly turf aeration. Then again, he might have put all his toys in the canyon. He'll grab his own leash and beat you to the door at the prospect of another bike ride or hike, and be positively ecstatic about a game of keep-away. Indeed, give him enough exercise during the day and he'll happily sit on the couch and share your popcorn in the evening. He might even beat you to the bedroom when it's time—and he'll know when it's time. And remember, if you let him, he'll figure out how to get his own way and train you to accept it.

Siberian Pros and Cons

Siberian owners, of course, think Siberians are the best thing that ever happened to dogdom. But Siberian owners are, like their dogs, pretty smart. They understand that only very special people are equipped to be owned by a Siberian.

Breed Needs

Behavioral Issues

By far the most common reason for behavior problems in the Siberian is too little physical activity and a lack of mental stimulation. The Siberian is a working dog who needs to be engaged in mentally challenging work or play. Ignoring him, or worse, leaving him to his own devices, will produce a lonely, bored dog whose pent-up energy explodes into destructive behavior.

- If you want a dog who will dutifully bring you your pipe and slippers, then lie at the hearth near your feet, don't get a Siberian. He'll chew up your slippers, and the hearth is way too warm. Siberians are extremely intelligent and very independent. If you spend the time to train your Siberian well, you're more likely to have one who won't chew your things—and, if you make it worth his while, one who might obey you unless something more interesting is already on his schedule. Siberians are not sporting, herding, or lap dogs. They were bred to work in partnership with humans, not as servants to a master.
- If you want a dog to play fetch with, that's not a Siberian. A few will actually enjoy the chase, but most don't see the point in bringing it

back to you. After all, if you wanted it, why did you throw it away? And besides, sled dogs are not sporting dogs—they rarely carry things in their mouths.

- If you wear black a lot, or insist on a pristine house and car, the Siberian is not for you. Siberians shed twice a year. The spring shed is profuse, the fall less so, but it is still sufficient to clog the washer and kill the vacuum.
- If you're looking for a watch- or guard dog, a Siberian will not qualify. Oh, he'll watch, all right—he'll watch the thief come and he'll watch him go, but it's doubtful he'll make a sound or come to wake you up. Siberians are a very gregarious breed; everyone is their new best friend, even that cat burglar crawling through your back window.
- If you have a menagerie of smaller, furry creatures, or birds for that matter, in your house, the Siberian is not your best choice of dog. Back in the day, the Siberian's ancestors spent the summer hunting and gathering to feed the pack. Although today's Siberians are provided for by their human pack members, their prey drive is not diminished.

COMPATIBILITY Is a Siberian the Best Breed for You?

ENERGY LEVEL	● ● ● ●
EXERCISE REQUIREMENTS	● ● ● ●
PLAYFULNESS	● ● ● ●
AFFECTION LEVEL	● ● ●
FRIENDLINESS TOWARD SIMILAR-SIZED DOGS	● ● ● ●
FRIENDLINESS TOWARD SMALL DOGS	●
FRIENDLINESS TOWARD OTHER PETS	●
FRIENDLINESS TOWARD STRANGERS	● ● ● ●
FRIENDLINESS TOWARD CHILDREN 5 TO 15 YEARS OLD	● ● ● ●
FRIENDLINESS TOWARD CHILDREN 1 TO 4 YEARS OLD	● ● ●
FRIENDLINESS TOWARD CHILDREN 0 TO 1 YEARS OLD	●
EASE OF TRAINING FOR ACTIVITIES/SPORTS	● ● ●
EASE OF TRAINING FOR TRADITIONAL OBEDIENCE	● ●
EASE OF GROOMING	● ● ● ●
SHEDDING	● ● ● ●
SPACE REQUIREMENTS	● ● ●
OK FOR BEGINNERS	●

4 Dots = Highest rating on scale

BE PREPARED! Are You Ready for a Siberian Husky?

Before you get a Siberian, you should be certain you're really ready for a dog in general and a Siberian Husky in particular.

1. Are you prepared to commit the next 12 to 15 years to caring for this dog?
2. Are there life events in your foreseeable future that may affect your ability to care for a dog or force you to move to a place that doesn't accept dogs?
3. Do you have children? And if so, how old are they? Puppies require a lot of time and attention, so if your children are under the age of six, an adult dog is a better choice.
4. Is everyone in the family committed to having a dog? Owning a dog requires flexibility and accommodation.
5. Who will be the primary caretaker of the dog? This adult must be committed to the dog, not an ambivalent bystander who may come to resent being saddled with the extra work.
6. Does anyone in the family have allergies? Before you get a dog, spend time in homes with Siberians. Since the proteins in saliva and dander are the primary triggers of allergic reactions, you'll want everyone to hold or pet the dog and allow him to lick you to make sure no one is allergic.
7. Where will the dog live? Siberians are perfectly suited to living outdoors in a secure and comfortable kennel, but they do not do well left alone anywhere for long periods. Dogs are social animals who prefer to be inside, being treated as a family member.
8. Does your family have time to care for the dog? If not, are you in a financial position to take your dog to day care or have a caretaker come in daily to meet the dog's needs? If the plan is to leave the dog locked up in the garage or outside alone all day every day, you don't need a dog.
9. Is your yard secure? A fenced yard makes walking the dog easier in the middle of the night or when the weather is bad. Tethering is dangerous.
10. Do you plan to train your dog? The main goal of training should be to build a bond between dog and family and, in the process, teach the dog manners so he can be a confident, well-behaved pleasure to live with.
11. Is your personality conducive to dog ownership? Dog ownership requires understanding, accommodation, adaptation, and humor. If you are unwilling to invest the time and energy required to accomplish all of the above, don't get a dog.
12. Do you expect strict obedience? No matter how smart and trainable a dog is, he'll never be obedient if you don't train him. Still, don't get a Siberian— they are too independent to meet your strict obedience expectations.
13. Do you value a squeaky-clean house and magazine-cover landscaping? Don't buy a Siberian.
14. Do you think it's cruel to keep a dog confined at all times? Then don't get a Siberian.
15. Do you want to be owned by a clever, mischievous, affectionate beauty who will love you no matter what? By all means, get a Siberian!

Children and Other Pets

Children

His spirited mischief and zest for life make the Siberian Husky a natural with children. In fact it's charming to see the special appeal that Siberians and kids often have for each other. After all, Siberians are playful and happy-go-lucky, just like kids. Like kids, Siberians are messy—they never put their toys away, and they leave their clothes (hair) all over the house. Siberians are energetic and curious, just like kids, and Siberians, just like kids, love an adventure.

Siberians tend to bond with their families, rather than with a single person within the family. Yet a gentle Siberian and a respectful child can strike up a friendship that'll last for years. Whether they're playing in the yard or reading together, a child and his Siberian can be a marvelous thing when each dog-and-child relationship is considered individually.

Generally, Siberian Huskies are good with and for children. However, there are several issues all families should consider before purchasing a Siberian, or a dog of any breed.

- Eight-week-old puppies are surprisingly strong, wiggly creatures who can easily be injured falling off the couch or bed, or being picked up and dropped by a toddler. Supervise small children and teach older ones to play with the puppy on the floor.

- Siberians are high-energy dogs, especially when they are young. Although most Siberians are instinctively gentle with young children, some may not be. Those who are fine with older children may be too boisterous for children under the age of three. The earlier socialization of both dog and child occurs, the easier it will be to ensure that both learn to be gentle and respectful. The bottom line, though, is that no young child should ever be left alone with any dog, for both their sakes.
- Even the docile Siberian has his limits. Most Siberians are very tolerant of children, but being repeatedly teased, hit with a toy, or having his tail or ears pulled will eventually make any dog feel threatened. The typical Siberian will first try to flee, but if he's cornered and rescue isn't forthcoming, even the most tolerant dog may attempt to warn his tormentor. Understand this show of teeth or growl is not the dog's fault, it is the child's and the parent's fault for allowing the incident to escalate to this point. The dog should have a safe place of his own where children are never allowed, and if the dog doesn't like the children, the children must be made to change their behavior. Supervising and controlling the children and protecting the dog are the responsibility of parents.

CAUTION

Good Reasons NOT to Buy a Siberian

- Don't buy a Siberian on impulse. A Siberian is a lifetime investment that requires proper education and careful preparation.
- Don't buy a Siberian as a surprise Christmas gift for anyone! An unwanted dog is hardly the same as an unwanted tie.
- Don't buy a Siberian as a status symbol or date magnet. Yes, Siberians are showstoppers, but what happens when the novelty wears off?
- Don't buy your Siberian around Christmastime or any other long holiday. Holidays are too busy for you to have the necessary time to devote to your new dog's needs.
- Don't buy a Siberian to teach your children responsibility. You're the adult; the safety and well-being of your Siberian is your responsibility.

- Siberians will definitely not hang with the kids. Siberians who can be trusted to stay in the front yard playing with the kids are very few and far between, so children and Siberians must play together in a secured area. It is also your responsibility to make sure your Siberian isn't accidentally let out by children running in and out of the house. And children should not be allowed to walk your Siberian until both are reliably leash trained.
- Siberians will welcome your children's friends. Remember, Siberians are gregarious, and will be thrilled to see your children's friends. However, it is your responsibility as the adult to make sure your Siberian is not abused by them. Again, adults must always supervise children and dogs, and the dog must have an escape route to a place of his own where no child is ever allowed.

Other Pets

Most Siberians have a prey drive as high as any wild canid on the planet. They will search for, chase, and grab any small or medium-sized furred or feathered creature they have access to.

Dogs Siberians are team dogs, and as such, enjoy the company of other dogs in their own house or at the dog park. In fact, most Siberians have never met a decent-sized dog they didn't like. However, to some adult Siberians, very small dogs just don't look or act like dogs and should be viewed by the wise owner as potential victims of the Siberian's prey drive. If you already have a small dog, the Siberian may not be the best breed for you. Consistently socializing a Siberian puppy to a wide variety of small dogs of all ages may help him recognize small dogs as dogs, but once he is an adult, the Siberian should never be left unsupervised with small dogs.

Multiple-dog owners can attest to the fact that their Siberian thrives on the company of his dog friend(s), so if your schedule doesn't allow you to spend time with and exercise your Siberian as much as you'd like, you should consider adding another dog to your household. Generally, adult dogs of the opposite sex bond more quickly than a puppy and adult, but you'll still want to make sure the new dog's temperament is compatible with your lifestyle, and with your resident Siberian's temperament. After all, your current Siberian should not have to suffer an aggressive dog or give up being first dog to a more dominant newcomer. And, to avoid any possible future mishap you may want to consider spaying or neutering the new dog before you bring him or her home. Introduce the dogs on leash and on neutral territory, and supervise them closely for a week or two while you give your original dog the same amount of time and attention he got before the new dog arrived. And no forced sharing! Make sure each dog has his or her own food and water bowls, toys, and bed.

Bringing a puppy into your home will be a different experience. First let your adult Siberian get used to smelling and seeing the puppy in a crate, not in your arms. Then, with a helper, take both dogs for short walks. The adult Siberian's initial response to puppies varies widely, from loving tolerance to wariness. You can facilitate your current dog's acceptance of this new puppy by protecting him from the puppy's pestering and devoting as much time and attention to him as you did before. Remember that puppies tend to harass adult dogs unmercifully because they don't appear to recognize the body postures that signal that the adult dog has had enough. Properly socialized adult Siberians with good temperaments will warn the upstart with snarls, and unless the puppy is in danger, you shouldn't interfere. Adult dogs who aren't properly socialized, or who have defensive temperaments or a history of fighting, may use more aggressive behaviors, such as biting. In either case, make sure your adult Siberian has his own safe haven where the puppy is never allowed, and don't allow your adult to bully the new puppy. Don't leave the puppy unsupervised with your adult Siberian until you're confident the puppy isn't in any danger.

Cats Every Siberian is an individual. Some, when raised with or by a cat, will live peaceably with the cat through their entire lives. If you plan to bring a Siberian puppy into your home, you'll need to prepare the cat. Keep the puppy on a leash or in a crate until the cat has a chance to get used to his scent. Once the cat realizes the puppy is there to stay, he'll adjust his lifestyle accordingly. Your job is to teach the puppy to leave the cat alone, because the cat can inflict serious damage to his face and eyes. Supervise their behavior, sternly correct all attempts by the Siberian puppy to chase the cat, and understand that you'll never be able to force the cat to interact with the dog.

Then there are the Siberians who, when raised with a cat, get along fine as long as the cat never runs from them once they've become adults. And there are those Siberians who, no matter how they are raised, will go after every cat they see. Do understand that virtually all Siberians will give chase when they see a cat outside, even if that cat is their inside friend. So, although it is true that every Siberian is an individual, the breed is generally not your best choice if you're already a cat owner.

Rodents, birds, and other pets It is generally accepted that most Siberians cannot be taught to coexist peacefully with small furry creatures, birds, or livestock. The normally gentle and friendly Siberian morphs into a swift, cunning, and tenacious hunter in the presence of small animals in and around your house, including squirrels, rabbits, birds, and pocket pets. Adult Siberians at large have been known to go after sheep, goats, cattle, horses, and wildlife as well. Your job as a Siberian owner is to understand and respect your Siberian's innate behaviors, protect your children's hamsters and parakeets, and never allow your Siberian to run loose. Although there may be exceptions, they are few and far between, because even today's Siberian's prey drive remains very strong.

Siberian Health and Longevity

Today's sled dogs are nature's ultra-athletes, possessing physiological attributes no other animal on the planet can match. They came by those attributes honestly, via centuries of natural selection for survival followed by centuries of selective breeding for temperament, endurance, and work ethic. Let's face it, the Chukchi couldn't afford to feed dogs who fought, carried their harnesses (didn't work hard), or couldn't go the distance. As a result, the Siberian Husky comes from hardy stock.

Every purebred dog comes from a closed gene pool, meaning that Siberians are bred only to Siberians to get purebred Siberians. Having a limited gene pool is both a blessing and a curse. It's a blessing in that one can be sure a Siberian puppy will look and act like his parents and have consistent, replicable, and predictable characteristics. It's a curse in that a closed gene pool increases the possibility that two copies of the genes that cause a particular hereditary defect will end up in one dog. However, this probability can be lessened by selecting a sire and dam who have been health tested and screened for genetic abnormalities.

BE PREPARED! The Cost of Owning a Siberian

Puppy: $350–$2,000 ($50–$300 for shelter or rescue dog)

Food: $20–$60 per month (including treats and chews)

Fence: $750–$1,500 and up, depending on size

Crate: $90 average

License: $18–$80 per year

Accessories: $20–$175 per year

Boarding: $35 per day average

Obedience classes: up to $100 per six-week class

Veterinary Costs

First year: (vaccinations, spay/neuter) $350–$600

Routine years: (boosters, checkups, parasite control) $250–$400

Senior years: $250–$400, assuming no major problems

Cost of a typical illness: $160–$500 and up

Costs in large metropolitan areas will be higher than in rural areas.

All breeds of dogs have the potential to produce hereditary problems, but the very few disorders seen in the Siberian, including hip dysplasia, juvenile cataracts, and X-linked progressive retinal atrophy, occur so infrequently that they can, for the most part, be avoided by choosing a good breeder.

The senior Siberian usually remains healthy well into his teens, especially if he is fed properly and kept in good physical condition, and it is not at all uncommon to find a Siberian living well into his late teens. The breed is not typically predisposed to develop "old dog" ailments such as peripheral vestibular syndrome (loss of balance caused by inflammation of the nerves connecting the inner ear and the cerebellum) or Cushing's syndrome, though particularly hardworking Siberians may develop joint stiffness in their later years. Regular checkups will help discover your senior Siberian's small ailments before they become major problems.

A Life-Long Commitment

Your decision to get a Siberian is not something to be taken lightly or impulsively. There are thousands of Siberians whose lives are snuffed out prematurely because their owners failed to live up to their end of the contract all dog owners agree to when they bring a dog into their home. So please, get a Siberian only if you are committed to caring for him, providing for him, and nourishing his spirit his entire life.

10 Questions About Siberian Breed Characteristics

Are Siberians good watch-dogs? Siberians are alert but friendly dogs who have no fear or suspicion of strangers. They aren't territorial, so they don't have guarding instincts. A Siberian may run to the door if he hears someone approaching, but is unlikely to give even a warning bark. It's often said that Siberians will cheerfully welcome the burglar, and might help him carry off his loot. This is not the temperament of a watchdog, though his wolfish looks may be a deterrent. They've been bred for generations to be friendly towards human beings and other dogs because an aggressive dog is not a good team dog.

Why don't Siberians bark? Siberians are rather quiet dogs who can but typically don't bark, yet can be quite vocal. They yodel, whine, woo-woo, trill, chirp, and howl. And they can howl quite well. Owners of multiple Siberians can attest to frequent group howls which seem to start and stop simultaneously. Why do Siberians howl? They are primitive dogs who howl to help reunite the pack/family, to welcome when the pack/family is reunited, to signal play time, and to express happiness and boredom. Some will howl just to howl, producing the most haunting sounds; music to the ears of a Siberian and the Siberian fancier, but maybe not to the neighbors.

Are Siberians part wolf? No. The Siberian is a primitive but domesticated pure-bred dog and has been for many centuries. Siberians are sometimes mistaken for wolves, and occasionally depict wolves in movies, but they are most certainly **not** wolves or part wolf. Siberians resemble wolves because they're genetically, like ALL dogs, closely related to wolves, but more importantly because they evolved in arctic Siberia. The Siberian's observable characteristics are nature's best answer to the arctic environment. He didn't evolve much beyond his original phenotype because most variations could not have survived. Today's Siberian remains close to his original phenotype, though it has been manipulated over centuries to allow him to live with humans and work in harness.

Are Siberians high-strung? If you define 'high-strung' as a dog who barks easily, can't adapt to a change in environment, is suspicious of strangers, and snaps or bites in fear, then, no. In fact, the Siberian is often described as even-tempered, laid back, mellow, and warm. These dogs are devoted to their families, but they are also excellent hosts when guests come over, rarely barking or acting territorial. However, Siberians are energetic working dogs. They need an outlet for their energy. When Siberians are lonely or bored, they can become destructive, so it's important to provide plenty of attention and exercise.

Are Siberians easy to train? Though very intelligent, Siberians can be one of the more difficult breeds to train, not because they don't understand what you want, but because, for their own good reasons, they don't want to do what you're asking. They don't readily take to jobs they have no interest in, but give a Siberian a job he is bred for and he will excel. The precision of competitive obedience exercises holds no interest for most

Siberians and it takes a truly dedicated owner to achieve high scores and advanced titles. This doesn't mean the Siberian can't be trained to be a polite house dog or an Obedience Trial Champion. He can, if he gets adequate exercise, companionship, and training.

 What about the Siberian's prey drive? Siberians fended for themselves during the summer in arctic Siberia, surviving for centuries by hunting and catching spawning salmon. These predatory instincts are still strong and have to be respected. While the Siberian is gentle and friendly with people and most other dogs, owners must be aware that livestock, small dogs, rabbits, birds, and other small, furry creatures are potential victims of their prey drive. If you have livestock or animals in your home or nearby, you have to make an effort to protect them.

 Are Siberians really escape artists? The Siberian has been called the Hairy Houdini of the dog world. They are pack oriented and if their pack goes off to work and school, the Siberian is alone. Lonely Siberians will eventually look for something to do, and that something may be on the other side of the fence; when something on the other side of the fence or window catches their eye, they will naturally want to check it out. When left alone for long periods, most need completely enclosed kennels on concrete to keep them safe outside. Inside, a sturdy metal crate should keep your Siberian safe and secure.

 Will neutering/spaying keep my Siberian from running away? No. The Chukchi routinely neutered their dogs, so the vast majority of Siberians imported to Alaska were neutered males. Thus, we know the Siberian's insatiable desire to run is not instilled by hormones, but is in the Siberian's DNA. Spaying or neutering your dog will not change his genetic makeup. Siberians were bred to lean into their harnesses, to go for hundreds of miles, and run and run and run.

Is it true that Siberians are not loyal? Yes and No. Siberians have strong affection for their human families, but they are rarely one-man dogs. Most arctic dogs are not slavish in their affections and some interpret this as a lack of loyalty. It is, but it's also a survival trait dating back to the breed's origins in nomadic communities where people came and went frequently. A dog who would not work for any community member because of his loyalty to one didn't stay around long. And this trait continues to serve the Siberian well in today's busy world.

What about destructiveness? Any breed can dig to bury a bone or chew up your favorite shoes, but no other can match the Siberian's landscape artistry. Dogs dig to find food, to create a den, to expose cool dirt to lie in, or to escape. Siberians also dig for fun and they can redesign an entire yard in a matter of hours. Digging, like running, is an innate characteristic of the breed which can be controlled but never totally eliminated. Assign him an area of the yard to dig in, or build him a digging box, but don't leave him unsupervised long enough to dig a hole the size of an Olympic pool!

Chapter Three

How to Choose a Siberian Husky

When you get right down to it, the most important reason for getting a dog should be because you want a pet. True, you might have plans for him to hike or bike with you, to show or track, or even to skijor—but first and foremost, you should want your dog as a companion, because there may come a day when, for whatever reason, either you or your Siberian chooses not to participate in sports anymore. He'll still need you and you'll still need him.

Three Absolute Musts

If you are planning to acquire your Siberian from a rescue organization, you'll most likely be willing to take the dog who needs you the most, and you probably won't have access to your new dog's background anyway. But if you're purchasing your new dog from a breeder, your expectations are different. You want a healthy Siberian with correct temperament who will be with you for years and years. To better your chances of getting such a dog, genetic health, proper birth environment, and correct temperament in the dam, sire, and siblings must be at the top of your list of required characteristics.

1. **Genetic Health:** Any living individual can become ill or experience an unforeseen genetic problem, but good breeders do their level best to avoid perpetuating known hereditary problems by screening potential parents. The serious Siberian breeder has at his disposal screening tests for hip dysplasia, juvenile cataracts, and X-linked progressive retinal atrophy. The prospective puppy buyer should inquire about these test results.
2. **Birth Environment:** So much of what one can see in a dog at 18 months is determined by where he was born and how he was raised during his formative weeks. A physically healthy dog is the result of a healthy mother, a parasite-free, clean environment, wholesome food, and appropriate physical exercise. A mentally healthy dog is the result of a mentally healthy dam and sire, a healthy and stimulating environment, and proper socialization.

3. **Correct Temperament:** A dog's parents are the largest determining factor of any dog's temperament—great parents beget correct temperament. Although a dog's personality is the result of both acquired and learned behavior, no amount of socialization will correct an inherited temperament problem.

You can be certain your perfect Siberian will be found at the home of someone who values the mental and physical health of the breed, fulfills his/her responsibilities to every dog, and is very, very picky about the homes the dogs go to.

Setting Priorities

On your list of characteristics after genetic health, proper birth environment, and correct temperament comes personal preferences such as age, sex, and type, as in performance dog, show dog, or pure companion.

Do you want a puppy or an adult? Most people automatically think in terms of puppies when they decide to get a dog, but you should consider the advantages of getting an older puppy or adult dog. For example, if your situation doesn't allow for the time it will take to deal with training an eight-to-ten-week-old puppy, you should think about getting an older puppy or adult dog. Many older puppies/adults are often already house- and crate trained, leash trained, vaccinated, and spayed or neutered. If you are interested in acquiring a competition dog to show or race, an older puppy or adult dog may be your best bet for a couple of reasons. First, it's almost impossible to predict at eight or ten weeks what the dog will look like at two years of age. Although most breeders have a good idea how their bloodlines grow, no breeder can guarantee that a given puppy will have the structure to race competitively or the characteristics to win in the show ring. At eight months or older, the puppy/adult will not be mature, but you'll be able to see major structural flaws and whether his shoulders and leg length are suitable for your purposes. And although virtually all Siberian puppies are active and playful, the successful competition dog has that special spark, often not detectable in a young puppy, that becomes evident in the older dog. Siberians are generally not one-man dogs, and adapt easily to a change in ownership. The one disadvantage of acquiring an older puppy or adult is that his basic character and emotional makeup was set by the time he was 16 weeks old. Still, if you like his personality, that's no longer a disadvantage.

Do you want a male or female? Both male and female Siberians are affectionate and outgoing. Males tend to be a bit larger and heavier, standing up to 23.5 inches (58.75 cm) and weighing up to 55 pounds (24.75 kg). Females weigh between 30 and 45 pounds (13.5–20 kg) and stand up to 22 inches (55 cm) tall. Males want to lift their leg on every light pole in sight and on your favorite shrubs, and neutering may not cure this habit. Females come in season twice a year, a sometimes messy nuisance that can be cured by spaying if you have no plans to show your Siberian in conformation. If you already have a dog, seriously consider getting a Siberian of the opposite sex, and spay and neuter both.

And finally, what are your plans for your dog? Do you want a performance dog, a show dog, or a companion to walk around the block with you every day? If you're planning to compete with your dog in performance events such as sledding, skijoring, or agility, structure should be a major consideration. The conditioning required to compete in sledding and skijoring, and the jumping required in agility, demand structural soundness, and although dogs who aren't sound can excel in performance events, how long they can hold up is always the question. Likewise, if you plan on acquiring a show dog, he must not only be sound, but also have the head style, coat, movement, and other elements necessary to win in the conformation ring. If the Siberian you're looking for is not destined to be your running mate in marathons or a big winner in the show ring, he can have a few structural or aesthetic flaws, but you still want a healthy companion.

All Colors from Black to Pure White

Siberians really do come in all colors from solid black to pure white, and in varying shades and mixtures of black, gray, and red. A variety of markings on the head and striking patterns on the body are a hallmark of the breed, which, when coupled with the wide range of color, ensure that no two Siberians are identical. But because the Siberian standard allows all colors from solid black to pure white, and there are no fatal or crippling color genes in the arctic breeds, serious breeders don't concern themselves with color. Below is a brief primer on Siberian coat color and markings, but remember that both can change dramatically between puppy and adulthood. There's no guarantee that the look you've seen and loved in an adult will be available in a puppy, or that the markings that caught your eye in a puppy will still be evident when that puppy matures.

Coat Markings

Irish Markings Siberians who have a mask of any sort, and white underparts and legs, are said to have "Irish markings." The vast majority of Siberians have Irish markings because such markings are genetically dominant over all other marking factors.

Neck Markings These are white markings on the neck that can vary in size from a small spot to a full shawl or mantle. The neck marking factor is dominant over both the white and piebald factors.

Piebald Also known as "pinto." Specifically, piebald markings denote white on the neck and rump area, but usually the white extends far up the sides. In fact, piebald may be used to indicate a white dog with black ears, but piebald dogs usually have black, red, or gray spots of varying size elsewhere on their bodies.

White White extends itself over the entire coat, resulting in a pure white dog when homozygous. Points (nose, lips, and eye rims) may be flesh colored, liver, or black. The other type of white Siberian, the Isabella White, is actually a bleached blonde. Isabellas occur when the black gene is oxidized into yellow or white. Buff saddles and ears are sometimes visible. Points are usually black, but may be flesh colored or liver.

Masks

Capped or heart shaped Color extends down the face to the eyebrows and around the sides of the head. A point of color extends between the eyes to form the center of the heart.

Cloverleaf Color extends over the head in front of the ears, forming arcs around the eyes and around the sides of the head. A white strip spreads up the brow, between the eyes, and onto the top of the head to form the third leaf of the three-leaf clover.

Open-face Very little, if any, color extends down the forehead in front of the ears, and very little color can be seen down the sides of the head.

Spectacles The eyes are ringed with color. This is often seen in puppies, but tends to fade as the dog matures.

Bar or stripe The point of color between the eyes extends down the muzzle, in some cases all the way to the nose leather. Width of bar or stripe varies. Most often seen on dogs with heart-shaped masks.

Dirty face Coat color extends onto the face. Some have no white on their faces, some have white cheeks and eyebrows, and in some, the color extends just onto the muzzle and below the eyes, forming sharp points. Usually seen in dogs who possess the genes for a full allowance of color and little dilution factor. They may also have black nails.

Coat Colors and Shades

Black and White

Jet Black Guard coat is solid black, and the individual guard hair is monochrome (not banded) black from root to tip. Single white guard hairs appear occasionally. Undercoat is black or more frequently dark gray. The jet black coat is frequently accompanied by great depth of black pigment on pads, nails, and roof of mouth. Often color extends far down the legs and chest.

Black Guard hairs are banded with some amount of white near roots. Single white guard hairs appear more frequently. Undercoat may be lighter than is seen in the jet black coat. Some buff-colored hairs may be found on lower stifle and in the vicinity of the ears. The dog gives the impression of having a black-and-white coat but without the depth of pigmentation found in the jet-black-and-white coat. Irish markings.

Dilute Black Guard hairs are banded, with the whitish cast extending substantially from the root and tipped with black. Undercoat has a whitish cast. Dog appears to be black on head and along spine while shorter guard coat along flanks produces a silver effect. Irish markings.

Gray and White

Silver Gray Guard hair is banded with various tones of white and minimal black tipping. The undercoat has a whitish cast. The effect is a silver shade of gray on head, back, and flanks, with only minimal darkening along spine. Irish markings.

Gray The guard hair is banded with cream and/or buff tones near the root with black tipping. The light undercoat gives the dog a yellowish-gray cast. Irish markings.

Wolf Gray The guard hair is banded with buff tones near the root and tipped with black. The cream tones in the undercoat give the dog a brownish-gray cast. A full allowance of the agouti gene produces warm shades of beige, tan, yellow, or red behind the ears, above the hocks, and in the saddle area. It is a full, rich color. Irish markings.

CAUTION

Rare Colors

The Siberian standard specifically states that all colors from black to pure white are allowed, meaning there really aren't any "rare" colors or patterns, just less common ones. Siberians can and do come in a wide range of colors and shades of colors. In fact, no two Siberians will be identical in color and markings because of the number of genes involved in producing the coat color, coat markings, and mask. Beware of the breeder who chooses to focus on color in his breeding program, because he does so at the cost of much more important traits. Color is the least important factor in producing a high-quality animal.

Red and White Always associated with liver points and complete absence of black hairs. Shades from mahogany to almost pink are determined by allowance of pigment, the amount of solid color banding on guard hairs, and the color of the undercoat. Irish markings are most common. Red dogs will have either amber or blue eyes.

Sable and White Always associated with black points and black tipping on the guard hairs. The guard hairs are always banded with red at the root and black at the tip. The undercoat is always red, orange, or chocolate—never beige, cream, or buff. Sables are very uncommon, as the mode of transmission is not known. Some Sables are born almost wolf gray and the red tones deepen with age. Irish markings.

Agouti Also known as "wild coloring." Agouti is an exacting coat color requiring special masks and markings. Any white markings are always cream. Color extends far down on the body and legs, often down to the toes, with no dilution factors present. The undercoat is charcoal. The guard hairs are always banded at the root and tip with black, at the center with yellow. A grizzled effect is usually seen in the saddle. Points are usually exception-ally black, whiskers are black and very stiff, and nails are black. The mask is always dark with a solid black bar down the muzzle to the nose leather. Agoutis are exceedingly uncommon because progeny can be of any color.

Eye Color

Eye color in Siberians has not been studied extensively. There appear to be several interacting genes with complex actions. It is generally accepted that brown is dominant over blue and bi-colored and parti is dominant over clear blue eye coloring. Color geneticists believe that a dog cannot produce progeny with eye color darker than his own, blue excepted.

Brown Dark to light, including an amber tone that is nearly yellow and seen in red dogs.

Blue White with a blue cast.

Bi-Colored One eye of each color: brown/blue; brown/amber; blue/amber.

Parti Portions of the iris color are different—blue with a brown spot; brown with a blue wedge; half brown, half blue.

The "Woolly" Siberian Coat

In Siberians, normal coat length is dominant over long hair, but there is a recessive gene for long hair that, when in its homozygous form, produces a long, silky coat, tufts at the base of the ears, a plumed tail, and feathering on the legs. This "woolly" coat is considered a fault in the breed and will be severely penalized in the show ring. It is not desirable in a working dog because the silky texture tends to hold snow and ice. Additionally, the length and weight of the guard hairs prevents the dog from opening up his coat to allow air to circulate near the skin, meaning woollies have the potential to overheat more easily.

Woolly Siberians, like their short-coated peers, are wonderful dogs—they just have a lot of silky hair, and owners need to be vigilant for signs of overheating when the dog is exercising. Woollies tend to matt easily, especially behind the ears and on the britches, and must be brushed often, even when they are not shedding. During shedding seasons, daily raking is required to prevent matting. Shaving a woolly will only make his already thick, silky coat even thicker and silkier, and lead to other problems.

Alaskan Klee Kai/Klee Kai

Although their standard is based on the Siberian Husky's official AKC standard, the Klee Kai is not a miniature Siberian (see photo below of an Alaskan Klee Kai). There is no such thing as a miniature Siberian. Klee Kais are a crossbred dog, derived from the Siberian and Alaskan Husky (a mix in his own right), Schipperkes, and American Eskimo Dogs. The Alaskan Klee Kai was officially recognized by the American Rare Breed Association in 1995 and by the United Kennel Club on January 1, 1997, and suffers from, among other things, extreme shyness, liver disease, Factor VII deficiency, luxating patella, and congenital heart issues.

Should You Decide on a Puppy

You can purchase your Siberian pet from many sources, but only the responsible, ethical breeder will be there for you when you need him or her. A responsible breeder will answer your questions and take the puppy back if things don't work out. Responsible Siberian breeders breed dogs because they admire the breed and want to contribute to its quality. They consider the puppies they produce to be their responsibility for the life of the dog, so they follow up frequently and stay in touch to know what's happening with their charges.

You want it all—a beautiful Siberian puppy with correct temperament and good health—and you have a better chance of getting that puppy if you go to a good breeder. A responsible breeder will enthusiastically discuss all the topics listed on page 42, and others you haven't thought about, in detail. An amateur breeder can discuss three or four, and the backyard breeder, who produces dogs for profit, not quality, doesn't know about raising healthy dogs.

Comparing Puppy Sources

All puppies are cute, and Siberian puppies are downright adorable. This very fact makes it hard to stay objective when you're searching for that special puppy. But that special puppy will be with you, ideally, for 12 to 15 years or more, so you'll want to spend at least as much time choosing a breeder and looking for your puppy as you would shopping for a new car or house. Your options:

Newspaper Ads Using classified ads from the local newspaper to locate a breeder is a gamble. Responsible breeders don't usually advertise in newspapers because they have no trouble placing their dogs. In fact, most people who advertise in newspapers are amateurs with little knowledge of the breed, who may not even know about their own dog's ancestry. If the classifieds are your choice of a source, first learn advertising terminology so you can understand the ad. Then visit without looking at the puppies to discuss the topics on page 42 before making a decision.

Internet Ads The Internet is the new and improved classifieds—new in that the anonymity of the Web makes scamming so much easier. For example, breeders who sell puppies through website services, rather than their own individual websites, may not even own a dog to sell. Improved in that you can look at more darling puppies online in an hour than you could physically locate and hold in a year! If buying a puppy online is your choice, make sure you

- call breeders on the telephone and speak with them directly.
- verify the breeders' physical addresses, and the names and phone numbers of people who have bought puppies from those breeders.
- search the Internet for the kennel names. See if they show up on a message board or forum. Then search the Orthopedic Foundation for Animals website to see if they register the hip and eye screening test results of their dogs.
- And finally, if you have any misgivings, you might consider setting up an escrow account so you can release the funds only when the healthy, happy puppy arrives with all his legitimate paperwork, the signed sales contract you agreed to before the sale, and health certificates.

Not all breeders who advertise puppies online are scammers, of course. In fact, many highly respected breeders have their own websites. The difference is that no reputable breeder will sell you a puppy without interviewing you first.

Companion Breeders Companion breeders typically have puppies available most or all the time. And although the puppies usually come with a 14-to-21-day health guarantee, there may be no mention of genetic screening of dam and sire. Companion breeders don't usually compete with their dogs, and some even go to great lengths to justify breeding "rare" faults and "rare" colors. Still, if companion breeders are your choice, check them out. Ask all the questions, see what questions they ask you, and make sure you're buying from a reputable source.

Hobby Breeders Not all hobby breeders are responsible breeders, of course. There will always be one or two bad actors, but for the most part, Siberian hobby breeders are passionate about the breed. The responsible hobby breeder's website, if he/she has one, is loaded with Siberian-specific educational information and links to even more. Photos emphasize the accomplishments of the adult dogs, and are often paired with sledding, obedience, and/or show records. This breeder usually breeds one or two

BE PREPARED! Topics You Should Discuss with Breeders

Ask every breeder the following questions:

1. How many breeds do you keep? It is the rare breeder who can achieve the level of expertise and involvement required to really breed for preservation in more than one or two breeds at the same time.

2. What genetic diseases affect Siberians? Responsible breeders know about the genetic problems, current research and current testing available to the breed, screen their own dogs, and have CERF or SHOR certificates on both sire and dam.

3. May I see copies of OFA certificates? You should receive the Orthopedic Foundation for Animals' (OFA) Dysplasia Control Registry certificates and X-linked progressive retinal atrophy certificates on both the sire and dam. Hip ratings can be fair, good, or excellent. Do not purchase a puppy whose parents have OFA ratings less than good; excellent is even better. Check the OFA website for the dogs' names.

4. May I see the pedigrees of sire and dam? If there are lots of champions, titled dogs, or dogs with race records in the pedigree, the puppies are most likely good, physical examples of the breed. Good breeders have the pedigrees in their heads and on hand, usually accompanied by photos and stories.

5. Do you provide a sales contract? Good breeders will provide a written contract clearly spelling out the terms of sale, the guarantees offered, and the buyer's and the seller's obligations, including a statement saying he/she must be contacted if, at any point in life and for any reason, the purchaser is unable to keep the dog. Responsible breeders will never shirk responsibility for dogs they've produced.

6. Do you provide health records and guarantees? Good breeders will guarantee the general health of the puppy for up to 21 days after you take possession under certain conditions.

7. Are you involved in dog activities? Even if you never intend to participate, a good breeder participates in some of the Siberian activities discussed in Chapter 7. Shows and performance events test physical qualities and natural instincts and are the only way a breeder can honestly measure his or her dogs against the breed's standard of excellence.

8. Is your litter registered? Good breeders register the litter within weeks of birth. Additionally, all the breeder's dogs should be individually registered with the AKC (or its equivalent in other countries). The United Kennel Club is the only other acceptable registry in the United States.

9. How many litters/puppies are available? Good breeders rarely breed more than one or two litters per year, in order to focus on those puppies and have the time to be involved in breed activities.

10. Why do you choose to breed Siberians? Good breeders work to preserve and protect the characteristics that make the Siberian unique. And good breeders understand that quality in any dog is a combination of breed type, health, soundness, and temperament.

litters each year, at most, specifically to better the bloodlines. The parents are undoubtedly dogs who have proven their quality in the show ring and/or on the trail. But even the most gifted breeder from time to time produces a puppy who will not be the next Westminster winner or Iditarod leader. This puppy will, however, be raised with the same care given his littermates, and sold to a qualified home on a spay/neuter contract.

Locating a Responsible Breeder

The Siberian Husky Club of America (SHCA) Breeder Referral Directory, available online at *www.shca.org/shcahp4f.htm*, is a good place to start your search for a responsible breeder (for Canadian breeders, go to *www.siberianhuskyclubofcanada.com/breeders/breeders.htm*). These breeders are members in good standing of the SHCA or SHCC, and have signed a Code of Ethics, agreeing to the following:

- To fully explain to all prospective Siberian Husky purchasers the disadvantages as well as the advantages of owning a Siberian Husky; attempt to help and befriend novice owners.
- To stay well informed in the field of genetics and work persistently to eliminate hereditary defects from the breed.
- To include, with contracts of sale, health records and guarantees, registration details, and accurate pedigrees.
- To provide proof that both parents are certified clear of hip dysplasia and X-linked PRA through OFA certification, and that both parents were found to be clear of hereditary eye diseases and registered with the Canine Eye Registry Foundation (CERF) or Siberian Husky Ophthalmic Registry (SHOR) within one year before the breeding producing the offspring in question.

In addition, these breeders will provide care, feeding, socializing, and training instructions; willingly answer questions as long as the buyer needs advice; and insist that the buyer agree to contact them should the buyer ever be unable to keep the dog.

If there is one near you, the local Siberian Husky club (*www.shca.org/*

CAUTION

Buyer Beware

Avoid breeders who

- have more than two breeds of dogs.
- will not allow you to see the dam and the rest of the litter.
- have Siberian puppies of all ages and colors available most or all the time.
- register their dogs with registries other than the AKC or UKC in the United States, or the national equivalent in foreign countries.
- advertise rare colors or miniature Siberian Huskies.
- won't provide a contract of sale.
- want you to take the puppy before he is eight weeks old.

shcahp4e.htm and *www.siberianhuskyclubofcanada.com*) is another source of valuable information. A local club will have events you can attend to meet breeders, see adult dogs, and find out about available litters. Should you live in an area where no local Siberian breed club exists, you can find nearby all-breed clubs through the AKC's Club Search tool at *www.akc.org*. The all-breed club's events, including shows, matches, or training sessions, are good places to meet Siberian owners and see adult dogs.

The Value of a Reputable Source

Choosing a breeder is every bit as important as choosing a veterinarian. You have your list of questions to ask all potential breeders, and you should know that the responsible breeder has a list of questions he will ask you. Good breeders have developed a profile of the suitable potential Siberian Husky owner because they are very careful about where their puppies go. Good breeders want to know why you want a Siberian because they know the breed requires a special owner. They'll ask about your experience with dog ownership in general and Siberian ownership specifically. They'll want to know if you're familiar with the zoning and dog laws in your municipality. They'll want details about your house and yard to make sure your Siberian can be properly confined, and may want to do a home visit. A responsible breeder will quickly figure out whether everyone in your family wants this puppy and who is going to be primarily responsible for his care. A good breeder will want to meet your children, and know about your lifestyle and your other pets, and may ask you for references. Your answers will help determine if your family and home is suitable for one of his/her dogs. Don't be surprised if the responsible breeder asks you to wait for a

litter—your answer will either confirm you're buying impulsively or confirm that you are serious about getting the right puppy for you. If a breeder doesn't care about where his/her dogs are placed, he/she probably didn't spend much time and effort planning for or raising the puppies.

Guarantees

Even if your puppy is sold on a limited registration or spay/neuter contract, responsible breeders will most likely want to have his eyes checked and his hips X-rayed, because the data is important for determining future research priorities. The only way to ensure that the lines don't have genetic problems is to screen for them. The responsible breeder will most assuredly have copies of health clearance certificates for the parents of your puppy, and probably most of his extended family members, so that he/she can feel comfortable guaranteeing your puppy will not suffer from hip dysplasia or X-linked PRA (Progressive Retinal Atrophy). Dogs affected with bilateral juvenile cataracts have not been used for breeding in decades, yet there are still dogs who develop cataracts. Dams, sires, and siblings for three generations or more have been screened, but there is no definitive way to detect carriers of the recessive genes responsible—yet.

Papers

AKC registration (or its national equivalent) simply means that the parents of the dog named on the registration are also registered as purebred dogs. Registration by itself does not address quality or health, only parentage, and by design, depends on breeder honesty. Very rarely does a registry verify the accuracy of a registration or send a representative to scrutinize the parents or the puppies. In the past, proof of mixed breeding was difficult to ascertain unless the supposed Siberian puppy grew up to look like a Great Dane. Today, DNA testing has given inspectors a powerful tool to ferret out dishonesty, but a DNA test for parentage does not guarantee quality or health.

Knowledge to Share

Responsible breeders are passionate about Siberians, and their lives often revolve around dogs. Reputable breeders feel responsibility toward the breed itself, the dogs they breed, and the people who have dogs of their breeding. They are active in their local, national, and/or international Siberian clubs and maybe the nearby all-breed club. Good breeders often participate in public education projects, Siberian rescue, training, therapy work, and canine health research. Responsible breeders will have personally seen generations of relatives of your puppy, and probably have photographs to share and stories to tell. The good breeder no doubt has an extensive library and bibliography to match, and will encourage you to become a student of the breed. Because the responsible breeder participates in Siberian activities, he/she can also help you get started in your chosen performance event or at least point you in the direction of qualified people who can.

Contracts of Sale

When you decide to buy that special puppy, you will want a written contract of sale that clearly spells out the terms of the sale, the guarantees offered and the conditions under which they are offered, all of your obligations, and all of the breeder's responsibilities. Sales contracts vary from breeder to breeder and breed to breed, but a well-written one will be designed to protect the buyer, the seller, and, most important, the dog. In all cases, you should check that the contract complies with your state's law, and agreements should be in writing. The following are common clauses in a contract of sale for a companion sold on a limited registration:

1. Establishes price and identity of the dog being sold. Identification includes the sire, dam, OFA and CERF/SHOR numbers, whelping date, AKC registration number, sex, and a description sufficient to distinguish the puppy from its littermates.
2. Lists vaccinations given, discusses the conditions under which the puppy was raised, and states the puppy's current health status.
3. Provides the buyer with a specific time frame to have the puppy examined by a veterinarian; provides an opportunity to return the dog within a specified time if he does not pass an examination by a veterinarian; requires buyer to protect puppy's health.
4. If the puppy is being purchased as a companion, the contract may provide that the buyer agrees to spay or neuter the dog within a certain amount of time; that the buyer understands that this dog is not intended for breeding and is being sold on limited registration; and that registration papers will be held until proof of spay or neuter is provided and exactly what constitutes proof.
5. Reserves the breeder's right to reclaim the dog, and under what conditions. Typically, if the buyer cannot keep the dog, for whatever reason, the buyer must notify the breeder. The specifics of what the breeder and buyer agree to do in this circumstance are inserted in this clause. Provides consequences should the buyer place, surrender, or sell the dog without notifying the breeder.
6. Statement that says if it's not in the written contract, it isn't part of your agreement. If both parties agree to modify the contract, changes should be written in and both the breeder and the buyer should initial each change before signing the contract. If you are planning to buy a show prospect, you should research show contracts.

Rescue

Siberians arrive in rescue for many different reasons, the most common being an owner's change of lifestyle. Some are neglected and thrive when they get the attention they need. A few have been abused, and a few come from puppy mill closures. Sometimes, entire litters are rescued, and sometimes litters are born while the dam is in foster care. Although it's true that many rescue dogs come with baggage, a rescue dog ready for adoption has lived with an experienced dog fancier long enough to have had his issues addressed. No responsible rescue organization adopts out a dog with serious behavioral or physical problems unless the adopter is qualified to handle them.

Siberian Husky rescue organizations guarantee the rescued dog a home for life, so everything possible is done to ensure the dog is properly rehabilitated and placed in a forever home. Thus, rescue services are not cheap, so rescued dogs are not free. Because all rescuers are volunteers, adoption fees, donations, and donated in-kind services are used exclusively on the dogs. All rescued Siberians are heartworm tested and on preventive, spayed or neutered, temperament tested, vaccinated, and microchipped before being placed in a foster home. Fostering families care for the dog as they would their own pet, providing companionship, training, and exercise, arranging for necessary veterinary care, and supplying generous amounts of patience and love. Fostering lasts anywhere from a few days to several weeks or even months, depending on the Siberian's needs. When he's ready, the rescued Siberian's behavior, temperament, and training level is again carefully evaluated so he can be matched to the perfect new owner. Potential adopters are asked to supply references and are interviewed in their homes. Adopters are asked to pay fees ranging from $125 to $300, depending on their location, and are required to sign a contract.

Helpful Hints

Rescue Resources

www.siberianrescue.com
Siberian Husky Rescue website with links to regional rescue organizations in New England, the Mid-Atlantic, the Southeast, Midwest, Southwest, West, and outside the United States.

www.petfinder.com
A searchable national database of dogs in rescue and in shelters.

www.srdogs.com
The Senior Dogs Project web page. Searchable national database of Siberian rescue organizations committed to helping older dogs find new homes.

Adopting your Siberian from a rescue group ensures you have an entire organization to help with any problems that might come up. You'll also have built-in opportunities to join your local Siberian Husky or all-breed club, participate in Siberian-oriented activities, attend rescue reunions, and,

CHECKLIST

Signs of a Healthy Puppy

Before you get attached to that little bundle of fur, check him over:

✔ His eyes should look clear and shiny. There shouldn't be any signs of cloudiness or discharge from the eyes. His eyelashes should not fold in on his eyes.

✔ His ears should look and smell clean. The inside should not be red, inflamed, or have debris in it.

✔ His nose should be slightly moist to the touch, but there should be no sign of discharge, and he should not be wheezing, sneezing, or sniffling. Gums should be pink, not pale.

✔ He should smell good and his coat should be soft and shiny, without flakes or shedding. Look for bald patches, redness, bumps, or scabs. Check for fleas and ticks.

✔ There should be no signs of diarrhea or fecal matter on his rear end.

✔ You should be able to feel his ribs, but they shouldn't stand out. His tummy can be round, but not swollen or potbellied.

✔ The puppies' area should be clean smelling and tidy. Look for signs and smells of diarrhea or vomiting.

✔ A healthy puppy may be sleepy, but should not be lethargic. You should see occasional bursts of energy and interaction with littermates. When it's mealtime, a healthy puppy will chow down.

of course, become a volunteer rescue member yourself. And you'll find it's true—rescued Siberians can be nice Siberians.

Picking That Perfect Puppy

Siberian puppies have to be the cutest on earth, but you must do your very best to first visit every breeder on your short list without actually seeing or touching a puppy. Instead, take your list of questions to interview the breeders, answer their questions honestly, and observe their homes and adult dogs. Remember, you're on a fact-finding mission, and you can find out quite a bit about each breeder by asking questions and observing closely. How does the breeder interact with his dogs? Are there dogs in the house, and if so, how are they treated? Do the dogs appear healthy and happy? How do they behave toward you? If you have the chance, check out the area where the adult dogs spend most of their time. Is it clean and well maintained?

Once you have shortened your list to one or two responsible breeders, you can start to make honest evaluations of their puppies. A responsible breeder, knowing you are coming, will have the puppies clean and as well rested as possible for their age. Puppies should have no discharge from their noses, ears, or eyes, and no signs of diarrhea. Although most puppies are a bit chubby, their bellies should not be distended.

Siberian puppies should be friendly, confident, alert, curious, and pretty boisterous at play. A six-to-eight-week-old puppy separated from his littermates may be a bit reserved initially, whereas the eight-to-ten-week-old will cheerfully jump all over you. Avoid the puppy who shies away. Depending on their age, Siberian puppies may charge around for a while, then collapse in a heap to sleep. You'll want to spend time assessing just how brash and independent a given puppy is and how his personality fits into your plans and goals for him. Are you gregarious and outgoing, or reserved? Does your chosen sport require a high drive, or do you want your Siberian to simply be a companion?

When Your Breeder Is Out of State

If the reputable breeder you've been referred to lives far away, plan on spending a lot of time on the telephone. You will need to ask all of your questions, and the breeder will interview you, perhaps several times. Assuming both you and the breeder decide the relationship is viable, you'll need to be very detailed and honest about your lifestyle so that the breeder can choose the right puppy for you. He or she has watched the puppies develop physically and mentally, and will have a good idea, based on what you've said, which puppy will best suit your situation. No doubt photos and videos of puppy and parents will fly across cyberspace as the litter grows, but if your breeder is shipping him, don't expect to get your puppy until he is 10 to 12 weeks old.

Puppy Aptitude Testing

One way to take a snapshot of a given puppy's temperament at a single point in time is through temperament or aptitude testing. Some behaviorists

Breed Needs

What Age Is Best?

Taking a puppy home before seven and a half to eight weeks of age, when the puppy is learning from Mom and littermates that he's a dog, may result in a noisy discipline problem. The good breeder will be gradually exposing the puppy to loud noises such as the vacuum cleaner, taking him for short car rides, and introducing him to new adults and children. Between eight and twelve weeks, a puppy needs widely varying positive experiences and individual attention, which can be provided by the breeder or new owner. He needs to meet as many people of all ages as possible, but play with children should be well supervised. So, the best time to bring a new puppy home is between eight and twelve weeks, but a well-socialized Siberian puppy of any age should have no trouble adjusting.

PERSONALITY POINTERS
Puppy Aptitude Test

Test Purpose	Test Construction
Social Attraction Measures degree of social attraction, confidence, or dependence	Tester kneels and coaxes puppy to him/her in a direction away from where puppy entered testing area.
Following Measures degree of dependence/independence	Tester stands and walks away, making sure puppy sees him/her walking away.
Restraint Measures dominance/submissive tendencies	Tester crouches, rolls puppy on back, and holds him with one hand for full 30 seconds.
Social Dominance Measures degree of acceptance of dominance	Tester in crouch lets puppy get up, then strokes him from head to tail until a recognizable behavior is seen.
Elevation Dominance Measures degree of acceptance of dominance when he has no control	Tester lifts puppy just off the ground with both hands for full 30 seconds.
Retrieving Measures degree of willingness to work with humans	Tester crouches and gets puppy's attention with crumpled paper ball; tosses object 6–9 feet (1.8–2.7 m) in front of puppy.
Touch Sensitivity Measures degree of sensitivity to touch	Tester presses webbing of front foot for up to 10 seconds or until puppy shows discomfort.
Sight Sensitivity Measures degree of intelligent response to strange object	Large towel tied to string is jerked across floor in front of puppy.
Sound Sensitivity Measures degree of sensitivity to sound	Tester, no closer than 4 feet (1.2 m), makes sharp noise—toy clapper or metal to metal works well.

believe that, if the puppy has been properly socialized and not traumatized before the test, temperament testing can be a good measure of the puppy's suitability for whatever role he is expected to fill and an excellent tool for placing puppies in compatible homes. Others claim the tests are not predictive of adult behavior, especially for arctic breeds.

The ideal time to do a puppy personality test is on the 49th day because the puppy's brain waves are the same as a mature dog's but the puppy's

What to Look For	Ideal Results
Does puppy go to tester eagerly, with tail down, or not at all?	Went to tester eagerly, with tail up.
Does puppy bound after tester, getting under foot; follow with tail down; or not follow at all?	Follows tester with tail up.
Does puppy struggle fiercely and bite; struggle and settle with eye contact; not struggle at all and avoid eye contact?	Puppy struggles, settles, and makes eye contact.
Does puppy jump up and bite, cuddle up and lick face, jump up and run off?	Puppy cuddles up or squirms a bit, and licks at tester's face and hands.
Does puppy struggle fiercely; relax without struggling; freeze?	Puppy struggles, then relaxes.
Does puppy chase, grab, and run off with object; fetch object; not go after object at all?	Siberians don't usually retrieve. May chase and chew; stand over; chase and return without object; not chase.
How quickly puppy reacts.	Puppy protests within three to six seconds.
Does puppy look, attack, and bite; look curiously and investigate; run away and hide?	Puppy looks and pounces; may shake or try to run off with towel.
Does puppy locate and walk toward it barking; locate and walk toward it curiously; cringe and back away?	Puppy may startle, then walk to sound curiously.

mind is still relatively free of experiences. Typical aptitude tests have nine different sections, and ideally are conducted by a person unknown to the puppies.

Chapter Four

Caring for a Siberian Husky Puppy

Your new puppy deserves the very best of everything —comfort, training, socialization, and safety. So before he even arrives, you've got things to do like puppy-proofing the house and yard, shopping, and waiting…and waiting…and waiting for the big day. Are you ready for your puppy?

Be Prepared

You've arranged to pick up your Siberian when you've got several days to devote to settling him into his new home. You'll want to have everything in place and ready the moment you walk in the door with your new puppy. You do not want to be without a crate, baby gates, or other necessities at six o'clock in the evening on the big day, so plan ahead.

When you go to pick your puppy up, you'll have a collar (not a choke collar), a leash, poop bags, and your puppy's travel crate with you. Before

SHOPPING LIST

Puppy Needs

- ✔ Collar, leashes, ID tag (flat, adjustable collar to rivet ID tag onto)
- ✔ Crate and pad (washable pad preferred)
- ✔ Food and water bowls
- ✔ Food
- ✔ Baby gates (to block off stairs/doorways)
- ✔ Toys
- ✔ Grooming tools and supplies
- ✔ Pooper scooper (for yard)
- ✔ Poop bags (for car)

leaving your breeder's home, consider letting your puppy and his litter-mates play with the crate pad, which can then serve to comfort your puppy with a familiar scent when he is separated from his canine family. If you intend, or need, to change your puppy's diet, make sure you leave your breeder's home with at least a week's worth of the food your puppy has been eating so you can gradually switch to the new food.

You will have planned the route home carefully, taking into account travel time, so that if you do need to stop to walk your puppy, a safe location has been predetermined. Make sure his collar is secure before you set him on the ground—remember, he may not be completely leash trained yet and he will be a bit frightened. Once he's home and it's time to feed him, you may be able to avoid nervous tummy upsets by feeding him a quarter to a third less per meal than what he is used to for several meals.

Diarrhea really plays havoc with housetraining, so you will want to be careful to prevent it, and, should it occur, stop it as soon as possible. If you haven't thought about or discussed with your breeder what to do if your puppy develops diarrhea once you get him home, here are some things to try:

1. Make sure you're feeding exactly what the breeder gave you or told you to feed, in the exact same quantity, except those first couple of meals. If the puppy was eating brand X performance formula and you're feeding brand X puppy formula, you've abruptly changed his diet. If your breeder told you to feed half a cup three times a day and you're giving your puppy one cup twice a day, he's eating too much at one time, resulting in diarrhea.

2. Check to see how much water your puppy is drinking at one time. Sometimes being separated from littermates makes puppies nervous and they drink frantically. Control his intake throughout the day, and if the weather is warm, substitute ice cubes for some water to satisfy his need for water. Chewing on ice cubes may help assuage his anxiety.

3. Don't feed your puppy table scraps or commercial dog treats until he's older. Dog treat recipes are very different from dog food recipes. Use pieces of his regular food as treats.

4. Have a stool sample checked for parasites, including coccidia and giardia. If it is negative, have another checked because, more often than not, parasite eggs and cysts don't show up in every stool.

Puppy-Proofing

Making your house and yard safe for a puppy is not much different from making them safe for a child, because Siberian puppies are much like children, only smaller. They are active, curious, and clumsy and must be supervised at all times. Check your home and yard for every poisonous substance and hazardous object or situation your puppy could possibly reach or get into. Lock up and put away clothes, shoes, tools, chemicals, medications,

CHECKLIST

Puppy-Proofing Your House and Yard

Check your house for the following items:

✔ Poisonous houseplants, candles, potpourri, air fresheners

✔ Swallowable objects such as coins, children's toy parts, paper clips, plastic bags

✔ Shreddable things, such as books, magazines, mail, newspapers, important documents

✔ Electrocution hazards such as electrical and phone cords, computer cables

✔ Strangling hazards such as drawstrings from draperies or blinds

✔ Chewable items such as remote controls, phones, CDs, VCR tapes

✔ Heavy things he could pull over on himself such as lamps, vases, unsteady tables

✔ Open fireplaces, ashes from stoves and fireplaces

✔ Accessible food, garbage, trash, wastebaskets, cans

✔ Open closets, cabinets, drawers, piles of laundry

✔ Swinging or unsecured doors

✔ Medications, toiletries, cosmetics

✔ Rags, sponges, household chemicals, detergents, antifreeze

✔ Craft and sewing items, paints, solvents

✔ Open staircases, decks, balconies

✔ Open purses, which contain sugar-free gum, lipstick

Check your yard for the following:

✔ Weak or broken fencing where puppy could escape, unlocked gates

✔ Access to a swimming pool, pond, in-ground birdbath

✔ Poisonous outdoor plants, flowers, shrubs, vegetable garden

✔ Fertilizers, pesticides, herbicides, rodenticides

✔ Hoses, rakes, garden tools

and razors. Keep out of reach poisonous plants, wires, low-hanging table-cloths, felt-tip pens, and insect/rodent traps and baits. It's easier if you get down on your hands and knees, so you see your home from your puppy's view, then go through it again, just in case you missed something.

Crate Training

Your new Siberian puppy needs a secure, quiet place of his own, a den of sorts. His crate is just that. When workers or delivery people are in and out of your house, he's safe in his crate. When you have to leave the house for a few minutes, he can't get into trouble because he's confined. When you can't directly supervise him, he needs to be in his crate.

Begin to associate the crate with good things by feeding your puppy in his crate the day you bring him home. Put his first meal just inside the crate door, so he doesn't have to go into the crate to reach it. Place each successive meal farther inside until you can close the door while he's eating. It won't take long before he runs to his crate when he sees his bowl in your hand.

Teach him to nap in his crate by putting him in the crate for just a few minutes when he's tired. After a playtime or walk, and only after he's gone potty in his designated spot, put him in his crate with a favorite toy for a few minutes. If he falls asleep, leave him until he wakes up and then take him outside immediately. If he doesn't go to sleep, let him out of the crate within a few minutes, preferably before he complains. If he does start to protest, wait for that one second when he's quiet before opening the door. Extend his time in the crate gradually, don't let him out until he's quiet, and always take him outside as soon as you let him out. Don't leave your puppy in the crate for long periods of time, except at night, while he is being housetrained. Bring the crate into your bedroom so you can hear him when he wakes up and needs to go outside.

Remove his water dish about two hours before bedtime to reduce his need to go during the night, but if your puppy does wake you up, don't make a big deal of it because he'll want to play and won't want to go back to sleep. Turn on as few lights as possible, and don't talk to or play with him—just take him out to his designated area, then put him back in his crate.

Housetraining

The key to housetraining your puppy is scheduling and prevention. If he is never allowed to go in the house, it will be easier to teach him to go only outside, never in the house. The best time to start housetraining your puppy is between seven and nine weeks of age. Before seven weeks, the puppy simply is incapable of controlling his bowels and bladder; after nine weeks of age, puppies want to use the surface they used between the ages of seven and nine weeks—the reason you do not want to let him have an oops in the house!

Puppies, like children, have an internal schedule you must live by to accomplish housetraining quickly and successfully. Puppies need to go outside the second they wake up, within 15 minutes of eating, in the middle of playing, a while after drinking water, and right before bed. And several other times in between those times. The younger the puppy, the more often

he will need to go because he can't hold it very long. With some exceptions, a puppy can hold it for as many hours as he is months old, within reason. At five months, he's at his limit until he reaches adulthood, when he will be able to hold it for six to eight hours. So, successful housetraining demands that you take him outside on a regular schedule and watch your puppy closely for signs he needs to go.

Using the Crate for Housetraining

By far, the most efficient way to housetrain your puppy is to use a crate. Puppies instinctively avoid soiling the area where they sleep and eat, so your puppy will naturally do what he can to avoid going in his crate, assuming it is not so large he can use one end for a bathroom and the other to sleep and eat. In such a case, you'll need to block his access to a portion of the crate. Your puppy should be in his crate whenever he is not being watched by you or another responsible person. However, he'll quickly give up trying to hold it if you leave him in the crate for long periods, so make sure you use the crate only when someone can't supervise him. Let him out regularly, and take him immediately outside to his designated area. And don't put him back in the crate once he's gone, except at night. Reward him with some playtime, but never leave your puppy unsupervised.

Once he's housetrained using the crate, enlarge his space to include an enclosed couple of feet beyond his crate. Treat this space just as you did the closed crate by sticking to your potty break schedule to prevent his having an accident here. Gradually expand his enclosed space as he successfully goes without an accident in it, until he has access to the whole room and more.

HOME BASICS
Your Puppy's Crate

- Do feed your puppy in his crate, as this establishes a good association.
- Do keep a safe toy or two in his crate to keep him occupied.
- Do keep him confined when he isn't being supervised to prevent housetraining accidents and for his own safety.
- Don't use the crate as punishment, as this will undo any good association he has with it.
- Don't leave his collar on while he's in the crate. Puppies can get their lower jaws caught in loose collars; hanging tags can get caught in crate wires.
- Don't leave him in the crate for long periods, as languishing can cause behavior problems.

Training Your Siberian to Go Outside

As soon as possible after bringing your puppy home, introduce him to his designated potty area outside. Keep treats by the door, so you can have one in your hand every time you carry him outside. Take him out through the same door every time. Supervise him and praise and treat immediately when he goes. Don't let him play until he goes. Be patient, even if it takes 30 minutes! And do not shove him out and shut the door—he'll just sit on the steps until you open the door, then come inside and potty on the floor. Stay on schedule, taking him out every hour, after every meal, during play, and every time he wakes up. It's inconvenient for him to be interrupted to go outside, so make it worth his effort with instant praise and he'll soon associate his designated area with rewards. The more times he's rewarded, the faster he'll learn. And trust that, all of a sudden, he'll be housetrained and you'll forget how long it took!

Housetraining can easily be achieved without resorting to old-fashioned hitting, nose rubbing, or banishment. Accidents may happen if you forget to stay on schedule or aren't watching him closely enough, but understand that punishing your puppy will almost certainly derail your housebreaking efforts. First, puppies aren't old enough to understand they're doing something wrong, and will learn to distrust you. Yelling, hitting, or otherwise punishing a puppy will only make him fear you, and fearful dogs tend to urinate or defecate in response. And finally, if you punish very often, your puppy will eventually associate his going with your behavior and try to hide it from you, even outside. Instead of punishing, if you catch your puppy in the act, issue a sharp "No!" scoop him up, and take him outside immediately. Stay with him until he goes in his designated area, and treat and praise.

Paper training is not an effective way to housetrain your puppy, because, as was mentioned before, once a puppy turns nine weeks old, he will want to use the surface he used when he was between seven and nine weeks of age. It will take a long time to break the paper habit. If you can't be there to take your puppy outside often enough, use sod pieces instead of newspaper or pee pads. At least the sod will blend with the grass in his designated outside area, and may help teach him to go outside.

Siberian Husky Development

Puppies go through many stages of physical, social, and behavioral development in their first year of life. Although there's not much for humans to do until puppies are two to three weeks old, breeders and owners have a tremendous influence on a puppy's mental and physical health after that.

Socialization

Socialization is the most important process in your Siberian puppy's life, ranking right up there with proper feeding and veterinary care. So what is it? In a nutshell, socialization is introducing your puppy to and acquainting him with new things in a way that helps him learn to respond to and interact with these things appropriately and without fear. His genes control his potential; his experiences will shape his behavior. Good experiences will teach your puppy that a given situation yields good things, whereas a bad experience teaches him to associate that situation with scary things.

Well-socialized dogs are happy, friendly, predictable, and able to handle stress. Improperly or under-socialized dogs can often be fearful, shy, unstable, and sometimes even fear-aggressive—and hard to live with.

Your Siberian puppy accepts new experiences more readily between ages four and twelve weeks, when his ability to learn is at its peak. He is also programmed to go through a fear-imprinting stage from about eight to twelve weeks of age. If a trauma in this time frame is left unaddressed by the time he is 16 weeks old, his emotional makeup may be affected for life. Knowing that experiences have their greatest effect on a puppy's future social behavior during this time, the good breeder provides age-appropriate positive experiences such as handling, individual attention, new people, and household noises from the time he is born until you take him home.

Now it's your turn. Because he's 10 weeks old, you need to introduce him to new people, places, objects, and situations only when you can make sure the experience will be positive. Your job is to help your puppy see new things as potentially good things. Control the situation, don't overwhelm him, and expose him to as much as possible before he turns 16 weeks old. If he's already a bit wary of children and the first one he meets steps on his tail, his fear may become generalized. But if his first is a quiet, gentle child, he'll be less wary of the next child he meets.

A puppy kindergarten class can be a great place for puppies to socialize with other dogs and for owners to learn how to communicate with their puppies. Some veterinarians oppose exposing puppies before they've completed the full series of puppy vaccinations, but the American Veterinary Society of Animal Behavior supports participation in puppy kindergarten classes as long as all puppies in the class are veterinarian-checked healthy and parasite-free when they enter the class and are kept current on vaccinations. You will also want to observe a class or two to make sure the instructor carefully supervises and controls the class and doesn't allow more dominant dogs to bully others. You do not want your puppy to have a negative experience.

Socialize your puppy gradually to tolerate dogs and other animals, umbrellas, canes, wheelchairs, men with beards and people in hats, younger and older children and oddly dressed teenagers, strange sounds, and sudden, loud noises. Don't introduce your puppy to large groups until he's been socialized to small groups. And then, when he's 16 weeks old, are you finished socializing? Nope! Just as you will train your Siberian his entire life, you will socialize him his entire life. He'll need to keep meeting and greeting, going places with you, and sharing your world if you want him to have a happy, confident life.

Here's what you need to know about puppy development through the first year. Also know that Siberians are fairly slow-maturing dogs, so yours will be far from an adult when he is a year old. He'll look and act like an adolescent until he's at least two, and some bloodlines don't mature until they're three years old.

Newborns: Birth–Three Weeks

Physical Development
- Needs food and warmth, not capable of regulating body temperature until two weeks of age.
- Eyes open at ten to fourteen days, ears between two and three weeks.
- Baby teeth begin to emerge at three weeks.

Socialization
- Incapable of forming attachments, but is aware of direct contact; puppies should be held, talked to, and weighed daily. Avoid startling puppies with loud noises or sudden movement while vision and hearing develop.
- Some puppies may interact with toys at end of third week, so introduce novel stimuli, such as a plastic bottle, to whelping box at two to three weeks.

Behavior
- May begin to eat semi-solid food at three weeks.
- Totters around at end of third week, attempting to tussle with littermates.
- Able to howl at 19 to 21 days.

Canine Socialization Period: Three Weeks–Seven Weeks

Physical Development
- Eats more and more solid food, eliminates without dam's help; drinks water after four to five weeks.
- Can walk well, rough-and-tumble play, and run with littermates by six to seven weeks.
- Coat becomes more adultlike.

Socialization
- Learns to be submissive to dam; play with littermates teaches dog manners.
- Meets new adults and children.
- Begins positive training sessions at five weeks.
- Puppy's rate of mental development depends on complexity of environment. Breeder takes puppies two at a time for short car ride, introduces outdoors and household noises.
- Puppies get individual attention away from dam and littermates.

Behavior
- Learns to chew and shred; can learn simple commands.
- Climbs out of whelping box to explore; learns to play with toys; individual personalities emerge at four weeks.
- Enjoys interacting with gentle dog uncle or auntie babysitter.

Human Socialization Period: Seven Weeks–Twelve Weeks

Physical Development
- All 28 baby teeth have erupted.
- Vision and hearing are fully mature by 10 weeks.
- Growing rapidly; ears and feet look too big for body by 12 weeks.
- Quite agile; able to run well.

Socialization
- Will learn to transfer affections from dam to people.
- Basic character is set between seven and sixteen weeks; good experiences are critical.
- Becomes more fearful of new things, generalizes traumatic experiences between eight and ten weeks.
- Needs to learn to be alone for short periods.

Behavior
- Learns bite inhibition from littermates and humans. Give a screech, and when he stops biting your finger, replace it immediately with his toy. Don't punish puppy, and don't play games that encourage biting during this time.
- Learns to walk on a leash; learns basic obedience commands.
- With consistent training, can become housetrained as early as three months.
- Chews everything in sight.

Juvenile: Twelve Weeks–Six Months

Physical Development
- Baby teeth are replaced by permanent teeth beginning at four to five months.
- Becomes heavier in the body; skull widens so ears don't look so big.
- Eats ravenously, is a bundle of energy.

Socialization

- By 16 weeks emotional makeup is fully developed. Take special care that experiences are positive, but keep getting him out to meet new people, dogs, and places.
- Flight instinct period occurs between four and eight months, lasts two to four weeks—he won't come when called, may run the other way. Keep him on leash and give him lots of individual attention.
- Second fear impact period begins between six and eight months, made up of individual incidents. Avoid reinforcing fear behavior by petting or reassuring; better to ignore him.

Behavior

- Does not like being separated from his pack, but continue to increase his alone time. Give him interactive toys when he is alone.
- Four-to-six-month period is characterized by independence and willfulness. Owner is no longer dam substitute.
- Is stronger and more curious; check your home and yard again for hazards.
- Can handle puppy kindergarten as soon as 18–20 weeks.

Breed Truths

Chewing

All puppies chew, and Siberians don't necessarily grow out of this typically puppy behavior. You can mitigate destructive chewing at the puppy stage by teaching your Siberian what he can and cannot chew on, and keeping him confined when you can't supervise him so that he never has an opportunity to chew on your things. Give him a few toys at a time, and rotate them every few days so he doesn't get bored. Don't give him toys that look or smell remotely like anything he is not allowed to chew. No knotted towels, wooden spoons, old shoes, or stuffed animals (if you have children). If you do catch him chewing on an inappropriate item, take it away and give him an appropriate one. Give him Siberian-proof interactive toys he has to work on to extract food.
See Chapter 5 for more discussion on chewing.

Adolescence: Six Months–Twelve Months

Physical Development

- Attains his adult height by eight to ten months; loses puppy fat, but doesn't fill out until age two to three years.
- Puppy coat may shed out, but might be retained until dry and brittle.
- All 42 permanent teeth are in by seven to eight months.
- Both testicles should be permanently down by six to seven months. If not, discuss options with your veterinarian. Retained testicles are subject to core body temperatures, making them susceptible to becoming cancerous.

- Your female Siberian will experience her first estrus between six and twelve months of age. Your male will be sexually mature by around nine months of age, and showing interest in females in season.
- Needs more exercise to maintain his calm house manners.

Socialization
- He may be a flaky teenager during the second fear impact period (six to eight months), and negative experiences could have a lasting effect. Then again, he may be becoming a very confident young dog. Keep getting him out to experience new places and people, and if he acts fearful, ignore him.

Behavior
- Older dogs start to become less tolerant of his puppylike behavior. Don't let them bully him, but he needs to learn the ground rules soon.
- He may test your authority. Deal with him fairly but firmly, and guide him to appropriate behavior.
- He begins to show signs of adult reasoning and memory capability at around eight to ten months of age. If you have plans for him, such as therapy work, sledding, or showing, he needs to be in training at this stage.
- Your male Siberian will start to lift his leg at about 10 months of age. Watch him carefully, because if he does it in the house, it is a difficult habit to break. If you catch him in the act, issue a sharp "No!" and haul him outside quickly. Females urinate more often during estrus.

Puppy Health

Health, of course, means more than just freedom from disease. In the case of your Siberian puppy, his safety, nutrition, level of parasite control, and veterinary care will all have an effect on his health.

Nutrition

If you purchased your puppy from a reputable breeder, he or she will have sent you home with detailed feeding instructions and at least a week's supply of the food your Siberian puppy is used to eating. If not, read Chapter 6 and avoid foods made especially for puppies, as their protein levels are too low for Siberian puppies. Also avoid foods that use soy, milk, or whey ingredients. Siberian puppies need twice the calories per pound of body weight as an adult

dog. Thus, they need to be fed all the food they want twice a day until they are about three to four months old. Young puppies tend to inhale their food, so there'll be less chance of him actually choking if you soak his dry food in warm water until it's mushy.

Puppies four months and older should be fed measured portions twice a day. Depending on activity level and growth rate, adjust the amount at each meal to maintain optimum body condition. Adolescent males tend to need a lot more food than females, and spayed females tend to need less food than intact females.

Vaccinations

Your puppy got his initial immunity to disease via the placenta before he was born and from his mother's milk during his first two days of life. There is no way of knowing how long his maternal immunity lasts, but it is known that maternal immunity interferes with the ability of a vaccination to stimulate immunity. It is widely accepted that the age at which puppies are able to respond to a vaccine and develop immunity covers a wide period of time. Research shows that less than 50 percent of puppies will respond at six weeks; 75 percent at nine weeks; 90 percent at twelve weeks; and close to 100 percent at fourteen to sixteen weeks. What is known for certain is that as your puppy's maternal immunity levels fall, his susceptibility to contagious disease rises, and the trick is to leave him unprotected for as short a time as possible. This does not mean that your puppy needs to be vaccinated with every vaccine that's available. See Chapter 6 for a discussion on the noncore vaccine for leptospirosis, and discuss the necessity and efficacy of other non-core vaccines with your veterinarian.

The American Veterinary Medical Association (AVMA) Council on Biologic and Therapeutic Agents' Report on Cat and Dog Vaccines has recommended that the core vaccines for dogs include distemper, canine adeno-virus-2 (use only CAV-2, not CAV-1; for hepatitis and respiratory disease), canine parvovirus-2, and rabies. State law dictates the age at which your puppy receives his first rabies vaccination; he'll need a second rabies shot one year later to be adequately immunized. Boosters for both the distemper series and rabies used to be given annually but are now recommended only every three years, according to the AVMA and American Animal Hospital Association. Check your state's requirements, as one or two still require annual revaccination and two states require bi-annual revaccination for rabies. Dogs in training classes and those exposed to large numbers of other dogs should be vaccinated against tracheobronchitis (commonly called kennel cough) twice yearly. So, if your puppy hasn't had one yet, and you're taking him to puppy kindergarten, he should probably have an intranasal kennel cough vaccination. Consult with your veterinarian to determine the appropriate vaccination schedule for your puppy. Remember, more is not necessarily better, and there are many different successful vaccination schedules.

Deworming

Your Siberian puppy should have been checked and wormed before you brought him home. You will want to continue to have your puppy checked regularly to catch any reinfestation. Most puppies are infected with worms, either in the womb when the hormonal changes of pregnancy cause dormant worm larvae to migrate through the placenta to unborn puppies, or through nursing when larvae migrate to the dam's mammary glands. Puppies can also pick up worms through contaminated soil.

All anthelmintics (medications that act to expel or destroy parasitic worms) are poisons, so don't deworm your puppy indiscriminately. And don't use over-the-counter wormers—they are often unsafe and ineffective. Have regular fecal checks done, and medicate only when indicated. Most heartworm preventatives also protect your puppy from other types of worms (see page 94).

The life cycle of most canine worms is such that the possibility of reinfestation is great. To keep worms under control, you must destroy the eggs and larvae before they reinfest your puppy. This means good sanitation. This means picking up feces daily. Year-round heartworm medication is effective in preventing intestinal worm reinfestation, so when your puppy is six months old, have him checked for heartworm infection and consider keeping him on preventative year-round.

Neutering and Spaying

The intact (not neutered) male dog experiences a huge increase in testosterone in adolescence, in effect jump-starting hormone-related behaviors, including urine marking in your house, behaving badly when there's a female in heat within a five-mile radius, and not eating or sleeping. He can't help himself, of course, because dogs are much more instinctive than humans. Twice a year, unspayed females wear britches or leave bloody stains all over the house. You won't be able to leave your unspayed female outside unsupervised for even a second because the scent of her urine will attract males from miles around. And then there's the possibility of a false pregnancy (pseudocyesis), when she will nest, mother inanimate objects, and maybe even lactate for up to 70 days.

The advantages and disadvantages of neutering/spaying before your Siberian reaches sexual maturity depend upon the sex of your dog. Once your male reaches maturity, he'll start marking his territory. The more he does this, and the older he gets, the harder it will be to break the habit. Spaying your female before her first estrus (heat) dramatically reduces her chances of mammary tumors or cancer, and eliminates her chances of ever developing pseudocyesis, uterine or ovarian cancer, or pyometra.

The disadvantages associated with neutering/spaying before your dog reaches maturity are also significant. Sex and growth hormones promote closure of the growth plates at puberty, so dogs neutered or spayed before puberty continue to grow, often unevenly, adversely affecting gait and causing increased stresses on the cranial cruciate ligament. Urinary incontinence, urinary tract infection, chronic vaginitis, and increased risks of hemangiosarcoma and bone cancer have also been cited as considerations. Many veterinarians who work with canine athletes recommend that dogs and bitches be spayed or neutered after 14 months of age.

Mistakes New Siberian Owners Make

1. **Getting a puppy when he's too young.** A puppy who is separated from his canine family before eight weeks of age could become a noisy discipline problem. He will have missed learning the species-specific behaviors that make him a dog and the effects of those behaviors on his siblings, dam, and other dogs. Most important, he will not have learned to accept discipline from his mother.

2. **Not supervising enough.** You wouldn't leave a human infant or toddler loose and unsupervised, yet Siberian puppies are very much like them. They can be gone the second you turn your back, getting into dangerous things you haven't noticed. A small puppy alone in the yard is in harm's way too. It is much safer to confine your puppy to his crate when you or another responsible adult cannot supervise him.

3. **Inconsistent housetraining.** If you want to quickly housetrain your Siberian puppy, you have to be vigilant and consistent. You can't forget to take him out every hour, when he wakes up, after he eats, and in the middle of play. Every time he has an accident, his training suffers a setback, so watch him carefully so he never has an opportunity to go in the house.

4. **Not crate training the puppy.** All dogs should be crate trained. All dogs need a place of their own to rest, to go when they need to escape from rowdy children, and to hide their favorite toys. Crate training makes housetraining much easier and faster. A crate keeps an unsupervised puppy safe when he is alone and confined so he can't chew inappropriate things. The best time to start crate training a puppy is his first day at home.

5. **Not using a crate in the car.** Loose dogs in cars are in harm's way. During an accident, your loose Siberian becomes a missile crashing around inside the car. If he survives the accident, he'll probably run in terror, and you'll never see him again.

6. **Not properly socializing.** If you want your puppy to join in all the fun when he's an adult, you can't isolate him while he's a puppy. Your breeder started the socialization process, and you have to continue to introduce your puppy to new people, places, and situations. If he is to reach his genetic potential, he needs mental stimulation and age-appropriate physical activity.

7. **Not using a leash.** Siberians, no matter how young or old, must be on leash or in a secure enclosure at all times. Your Siberian puppy could outrun you by the time he was six weeks old, and he'll only get faster. Loose Siberians are in harm's way, so never, ever take your puppy anywhere without his leash—that one dash across the road could be his last.

8. **Not securing the house and yard.** Siberians run, even as puppies. You need to make sure your Siberian puppy can't get out of the yard through a gap in the fence, or dig under the fence, or climb over it. You also need to make sure your puppy is in his crate or otherwise restrained when you or anyone else opens a door that leads to an unsecured space.

9. **Encouraging puppy antics not appropriate in adult dogs.** Your Siberian puppy will grow up. And you won't think it's so cute when your 50-pound (22.5-kg) adult Siberian launches himself across the coffee table into your lap. So, every time your little darling does something incredibly cute, imagine him doing the same thing when he's grown. It's easier to discourage these behaviors and teach good ones than it is to break your adult Siberian of bad habits.

10. **Believing everything that's published on the Internet.** By its very nature the Web, and the information found on it, can be informative, baseless, or downright dangerous. Before you believe anything you find on the Internet, check for documentation that it is evidence based rather than anecdotal opinion. Before you give your Siberian anything, such as a "recommended" supplement, talk to your veterinarian and breeder; before you implement anything, such as a "proven" training technique, speak to a certified obedience instructor.

Chapter Five

Living with a Siberian Husky

The Siberian has a zest for life unmatched by any other breed. He's good natured, affectionate, and friendly. He is the smartest, most beguiling, most beautiful, most nearly ideal dog known to man. Yes, Siberians are dogs. They look like dogs, they sound like dogs, and they do all the marvelous and aggravating things dogs do.

Free Spirit

The Siberian is a genetic parcel of innate behaviors that has taken several thousand years to refine, and although he is capable of being well mannered by human standards, he's a dog—he'll never really learn to say please and thank you or to clean up his toys. Being a particularly primitive dog, the Siberian's innate behaviors tend more toward the free spirit than the pipe and slippers. And although it's a fact that the Siberian's behaviors are governed by his genes, it is also true that innate behaviors can be directed with training or accommodated by the owner who understands why the Siberian does what he does.

Siberians Dig And dig, and dig, and dig. Digging is a natural canid behavior, practiced by wild and domesticated dogs, foxes, coyotes, and wolves. In the wild, this survival trait manifests itself as a den for raising young, or a cache to store food, or an enlarged chipmunk hole. Siberians dig up dandelions, or your favorite shrub, and eat the roots. They dig cooling holes to lie in in warm weather and dens to sleep in during winter. They dig under fences to escape. When they sniff out the presence of a small, furry creature, Siberians will excavate the entire yard, or the dining room carpet, if need be, to find it. Siberians also dig for fun, and although there are steps you can take to curtail one of the Siberian's favorite pastimes, you will never completely eliminate it. See page 79 for ways to confine this predilection.

Siberians Chew Just like human babies, puppies chew when they are teething. Unlike human babies, chewing behavior doesn't usually cease once the Siberian's permanent teeth appear. A young dog, especially the always alert and curious Siberian, will investigate novel items with his mouth. While he's investigating, the Siberian will rarely carry the object, but he may well lick, bite, gnaw, shred, and/or shake it until his curiosity is satisfied. Even adult Siberians will chew because they enjoy it. Make sure your dog learns early on what he can and cannot chew, and provide him with plenty of appropriate and indestructible items for exercising his jaws. Page 80 has tips for preventing destructive chewing.

Siberians Take Taking and eating any and all available food is the default setting for a normal dog of any breed. The ancestral rule is to cram in as much as possible, because lean times could be a-comin'! NOT doing so is unnatural and unusual for any dog who has not been trained to exercise self-restraint. Siberians are the ultimate survivors, and what they take, in their minds, is absolutely necessary for their survival. Food left unguarded on the grill, on the table, or on the kitchen counter is fair game to the athletic Siberian, whose genetic heritage tells him he can never quite be sure when he'll be fed again. And that container? Snatching and getting it open, even if it never contained food, is necessary to practice his survival skills. Although you can teach your Siberian to stay off the counter or table in your presence, it is doubtful he will pass up the chance to take off with the roast when you're not looking. And it quickly becomes second nature for Siberian owners to never leave an open, unattended grill where the dog can reach it.

Siberians Scavenge Biologists believe wolves first gathered around the campsites of Paleolithic man to scavenge refuse because it takes less effort and is far less risky to take advantage of another predator's kill than to hunt down one's own meal. Fast-forward several thousand years to your kitchen and nothing much has changed. The scraps you put in the garbage are leftover kill, and any self-respecting Siberian will take advantage of it. And what might man's best scavenger find outside the home? Nose to the ground, he'll scan for anything remotely ingestible. Delightful treats include long-dead remains and maggot-infested garbage. The stinkier this stuff is, the better it will camouflage your Siberian's scent when he rolls in it too! Putting the garbage under the sink is probably the easiest way to prevent inside forays; regularly patrolling the yard and keeping your Siberian in it or on leash is the only way to prevent him from venturing farther afield for some good old-fashioned refuse. And fence off that compost heap!

Breed Truths

Complex Emotions

Research shows that dogs do not have the brain function necessary for abstract thought; therefore, they do not experience guilt, jealousy, spite, or revenge. They are not capable of deciding to chew up your shoe because you left them alone two hours ago. Dogs live in the now. They can associate your praise or punishment with the behavior they are actually engaged in ONLY when you give it. A dog simply cannot associate the act with getting in trouble for it later. His guilty look is nothing more than submission in response to the look on your face. He has no idea why you're yelling. All you've taught him is that you're unpredictably crazy.

FYI: It's not just what you say, it's how you say it.

As much as we would like to believe that dogs understand every word we say, they don't. Phrases and sentences only confuse them. The tone of voice you use is as important as your words. Use these tips to more clearly communicate with your Siberian:

- Use short commands, one or two words at most. Instead of "Come on, Tavik, let's go outside and take a long walk," say, "Tavik, let's go!"
- Be consistent with the command words and the tone of voice you use. Instead of varying your tone each time, and saying, "Go lie on your rug," or "Please lie down, Tavik," always use "Tavik, down," in the same lower-pitched tone of voice.
- To calm or slow your dog down, use a drawn-out, quiet, monotone word like "E-a-a-a-s-s-y."
- Low-pitched, abrupt sounds such as "Ah!" or "Hey" will stop your dog in his tracks.
- Staccato sounds such as "Pup, pup, pup, pup, pup!" that continue to rise in pitch will speed your dog up.
- Use a higher-pitched tone of voice to encourage your dog.
- Use a lower-pitched tone of voice to issue commands.
- Shouting teaches your dog nothing.
- Repeating commands teaches your dog he doesn't have to obey the first one.
- Don't tell your dog to do something unless you intend to enforce the command.

Siberians Sniff It is often said that dogs live with their noses; they see through their sense of smell. Dogs communicate by leaving scents for one another, and Siberians are excellent at using their noses to keep track of what is going on in the world around them. Dogs can be trained to identify, or "hit on," specific odors, including those given off by insects, explosives, certain cancers, or a missing person. Dogs can "smell fear" by detecting the anal gland scent of a dog under stress. Sniffing the ground can signal "I'm minding my own business" or calm a barking dog as you and your Siberian walk by. A puppy will sniff the ground to signal that he is nonthreatening to an older, or strange, dog. As a puppy matures, he learns that sniffing the genital area can tell him what the other dog, or person, eats, his level of energy, his health status, age, sex, and much more. A well-socialized dog will allow this meet-and-greet sniffing; your neighbor most likely will not. Although an occasional source of minor embarrassment, your Siberian's nose is truly amazing, and he would literally be lost without it.

Siberians Guard Possession, in the dog world, is nine-tenths of the law. The concept of sharing doesn't exist. In human society, however, as far as the dog's possessions are concerned, what is ours is ours and what's his is also ours. The conflict between canine instinct and human expectation invariably leads to trouble if the dog doesn't learn early on that human rules apply. Siberians, thankfully, were not selectively bred by man to guard, so they do not exhibit the high level of possessiveness seen in some other breeds. Still, Siberians are primitive dogs, and their natural instinct is to protect their resources—their food and their toys. It's fairly easy to teach your Siberian puppy to relinquish his favorite toy or food bowl. See page 87 for advice on dealing with adult resource guarding.

Siberians Mount Dogs may mount other dogs, people, or inanimate objects for several reasons. Mounting is a normal, and not always sexual, behavior. Play mounting, like play fighting and play biting, is often seen. Older dogs, both male and female, also mount one another to establish dominance and submission. Medical conditions, including urinary tract infections and hormone imbalances, can contribute to mounting behavior, so a dog showing sudden or obsessive mounting behavior should be checked by a veterinarian.

Siberians Hunt Prey drive is the instinctive behavior of a carnivore to pursue and capture prey. Although selective breeding of some dogs has intensified or reduced one or more of the aspects of prey drive to suit a purpose—retrievers chase prey and bring it back to the human hunter without damage; herding dogs stalk and chase, but most do not wound their charges—the Siberian's prey drive is complete and balanced, though the level of drive can vary substantially from dog to dog. Given the opportunity, the Siberian will search, stalk, chase, grab, and kill. Your job is to channel his prey drive to more socially acceptable, productive activities.

Siberians Run Siberians have an insatiable desire to do what they were bred for centuries to do, and that's run. They love to run and will do so at every opportunity. Your job is to give them many opportunities to exercise with you and none to run without you. If your Siberian does get loose, don't chase him. Follow him in the car, and as soon as you get a chance, open the door. He'll most likely get in, and you will praise him lavishly for coming to you.

Breed Truths

Although the Siberian's good points far outweigh the bad, Siberians do have some innate behaviors that humans find aggravating or objectionable. This doesn't mean you have to accept those behaviors as unalterable. It just means you'll have to learn and work to change or redirect them, and that may not be easy.

Social Beings

In order to successfully train your Siberian and accommodate his innate behaviors, you have to understand what he needs. Siberians are very pack oriented—they are team dogs. They require the companionship of others, canine or human, and they don't do well left alone for long periods of time. This isn't to say that Siberians can't happily live as "only dogs," or that they can be happy only in homes where someone is at home all day. There is always a way to accommodate, if the Siberian owner is willing.

Siberians are social—they thrive on activity, even if it's just a car ride. And because they are so gregarious, they are easy to include in family outings. If he's been alone all day every day, the typical Siberian will probably not be content to sit on the couch with you night after night. After eight hours in his crate your Siberian will enjoy going out to the dog park or for a long walk so he can catch up on scent messages left for him by other neighborhood dogs. Obedience classes provide mental stimulation as well as socialization.

Siberians are graceful, agile, energetic, and athletic—they love to run. Some will say that Siberians think running full tilt, pulling a sled or skier, and carrying a backpack are their purposes in life. But they also enjoy agility, fly ball, or a good game of hide-and-seek in the backyard. Just about any type of exercise will make your Siberian happy, and a happy Siberian will be content to sit on the couch. If you give him what he needs—exercise, training, and attention—he'll be able to give you what you want: a calm, well-behaved Siberian.

Talking to Your Siberian

It is said that body language is a dog's most natural language. People can communicate through body language too, but more often than not, the body postures and movements of dogs and those of humans have different meanings. Dogs are not dumb; they simply have a world view so dissimilar that people aren't managing to communicate with them. Still, some dogs are able to bridge the communication gap despite human failings. You can help your Siberian by realizing how your body postures and tone of voice influence the way your dog understands what you're trying to tell him. Would a video show you

- **Patting your dog on the head?** In the dog world a paw on the head or shoulder is a sign of dominance. Your Siberian will probably walk away, or, if he's already submissive, lower his head and cringe. Find out where your dog likes to be stroked or scratched, behind the ears, on the chest, or at the base of his tail, and do that instead.
- **Hugging your Siberian?** People hug to give reassurance or show affection. To a dog, hugging is rude and most will try to pull away. However, you can't always protect your dog from an uninformed child or other human, so you do need to teach him to accept hugs gracefully. A treat as you give him a quick hug will ensure he associates human arms around his neck with good things.

- **Walking straight up to your dog, then hovering over him?** If you walked toward another person in an arc, he or she would wonder what your problem was, but that is exactly the way dogs approach each other; to face another dog head-on and invade his space is seen as a threat. Don't force your Siberian to heel up to a strange dog; he'll be uncomfortable. When you walk up to your dog in the yard, approach him at an angle, and kneel down to his level. Better yet, since you're the lead dog, call your Siberian to you.
- **Staring at your dog?** An unwavering stare can intimidate or frighten a submissive dog, and present a challenge to a dominant dog. Staring your dog down to bully him or as punishment is very different from teaching your dog to make eye contact for attention's sake. If you're correcting an inappropriate behavior, look past your Siberian or at his ear. When the situation calls for direct eye contact, keep it short. You should break eye contact first, then praise your dog.

Managing Behavior Problems

Typically, a behavior problem is defined as any behavior in opposition to the owner's expectations. Even normal behavior may be expressed inappropriately, depending on the environment. Whether the problem originates with the owner or the dog, nobody's perfect, and the fact remains that behavior problems are the number one reason dogs end up in shelters. It is unrealistic to expect any dog to always behave perfectly, and it's inhumane to allow a problem to escalate to the point where you think you have no choice but to surrender your precious Siberian. The responsible thing to do is deal with the problem before it comes to that.

Helpful Hints

An Ounce of Prevention

If your toddler repeatedly put oatmeal in the DVD player, what would you do? Sit him down and explain why that's not a good idea? Would you smack him every time he did it? No, you'd move the DVD player out of his reach. Ta-da! Problem solved. Prevention is usually the best solution, and when it comes to training a dog, the easiest way to deal with a behavior problem may be to simply prevent the undesired behavior from happening in the first place. If your dog raids the garbage can, you could spend weeks training a perfect *down-stay* in another room, or you could secure the garbage can. Prevention is also important if you're trying to train your dog to do one thing instead of another. An example would be housetraining your Siberian. He'll learn fastest if you use a crate to prevent accidents inside while you focus on training him to eliminate outside.

Excessive Howling

Howling is one of the Siberian's many forms of vocal communication. They howl to attract attention, to make contact with others, and because they enjoy howling. Some Siberians also howl in response to high-pitched sounds such as sirens and musical instruments. Your dog's howling becomes excessive when it results in neighborhood disputes and violations of animal control ordinances. Determining when, for how long, and why he's howling is the first step in quieting him. Quite often, simply isolating the reason for the howling behavior presents the logical solution.

Some Siberians howl because they get lonely when they're left alone for long periods of time with nothing to do. If your dog howls a lot when he's by himself, you may try to enrich his environment by providing Siberian-tested toys and chewing items to keep him busy. Rotating the toys every few days makes them seem new and interesting. You can also try spending more quality time together. Bring him inside more often, play games, and take walks with him. Take him to a fun training class, and take him to work with you every now and again, if that's possible.

Some Siberians howl because they are bored. These are usually the Siberians who need more exercise than they are getting. Long walks, runs, or bike rides before or after work may help, along with chew toys to keep him busy during the day. If you work very long hours, consider taking him to a doggie day care or having a professional dog walker, friend, or neighbor walk and/or play with him.

Some Siberians howl in response to sirens, musical instruments, and other aural triggers. He probably stops howling when the sound stops, and his howling isn't a problem unless the trigger occurs frequently. If this is the case, you'll need to do some detective work to find the trigger. Ask your neighbors, use a tape recorder, drive or walk around the block, and watch and listen until you locate the source. Ideally, you can make arrangements to eliminate the sound, or at least reduce its frequency, but if that proves to be impossible, consider keeping your dog inside when you're not at home to supervise him.

Aversion collars (shock, citronella spray, and sound correction) are not recommended for several reasons, the most important being that if they work at all, the results will be temporary because they don't address the cause of the inappropriate behavior. When aversion training is used without a plan to deal with the underlying reason for the excessive howling, the behavior may diminish but will almost always be replaced by another inappropriate behavior such as digging or destruction. If punishment is used when howling is a symptom of fear, anxiety, or a phobia, the underlying problem will only get worse.

Digging

Digging is a normal behavior for Siberians, and unless yours is never off-leash, he is guaranteed to dig for a variety of reasons—none of which include revenge, spite, or a true desire to destroy your yard, carpet, or couch. The instinct to dig is ancient, and although it can be curbed to some extent, it will not be eliminated. Making the hole your Siberian just dug unappealing may be effective in the short term, but the truth is, he's likely to start another one somewhere else as soon as he gets a chance. Most experienced Siberian owners will suggest providing your dog with an area in the yard where he is allowed, even encouraged, to dig, and training him to dig there. To teach the dog to dig only in the designated area, bury toys or treats, and encourage your Siberian to find them. Praise him and repeat until the dog willingly runs to the area to dig. Watch him carefully, so that when he starts to dig in any other place, you can dash out and take him to his

digging area. You might safeguard your landscaping and garden by fencing it off, but, bottom line, if your lawn and flowers are your pride and joy… don't get a Siberian.

If your Siberian digs under the fence to escape, well, that's a whole different issue. First, you need to keep him in the yard, which you can do in several ways. If you are installing a new fence, bury the fencing fabric at least 18 inches (45 cm) into the ground. If you already have a fence, you can bury woven wire, welded wire, or galvanized mesh horizontally at the base of the fence so that it extends at least 2 feet (60 cm) into the yard. Large rocks or fence posts laid horizontally and secured along the bottom of the fence line will work if your Siberian is not obsessive about digging out. If he is, and he's left to his own devices long enough, he'll be able to dig around or under the fence posts or rocks. Running an electrified wire along the bottom of the fence may keep him away from the fence if he's only occasionally left in the yard unsupervised for short periods.

Helpful Hints

Getting Professional Help

If your Siberian should develop a serious behavior problem, you'll need serious help, and a board-certified veterinary behaviorist is your best choice. Behaviorists work with individual owners and other animal professionals to provide the insight needed to manage the behavior problem and improve the dog's well-being. Veterinary behaviorists also have the advantage of being able to diagnose and treat medical problems such as chemical imbalances, epilepsy, brain tumors, and diseases that can cause behavior problems. Your veterinarian can consult with a veterinarian behaviorist or refer you to one in your area. Go to *www.veterinarybehaviorists.org* for more information.

Destructive Chewing

It's normal for puppies and dogs to chew on objects as they explore the world. For puppies, chewing relieves the pain that might be caused by erupting teeth. For older dogs, it's nature's way of keeping jaws strong and teeth clean. Chewing also combats boredom and can relieve mild anxiety or frustration. Dogs love to chew on bones, sticks, and just about anything else. Although chewing is normal, dogs sometimes direct their chewing behavior toward inappropriate items and need to be taught what is okay to chew and what is not. Here are some tips to protect your possessions.

- "Dog-proof" your house. Put valuable objects away until you're confident that your dog's chewing behavior is restricted to appropriate items. Keep shoes and clothing in a closed closet, laundry in a hamper, garbage under the sink, and books on shelves. Keep doors closed. Prevention is key.

- Provide your dog with plenty of his own toys and bones. Take note of the toys that keep him chewing for long periods of time, and offer those often. Siberian-tested chew toys and natural bones are good choices. Rotate your dog's chew toys every couple of days so that he doesn't get bored with them.
- Offer your dog edible things to chew only when you can supervise, because dogs can choke on edible chews, especially if they bite off and swallow large hunks.
- Identify times of the day when your dog is most likely to chew and give him a Siberian-tested puzzle toy filled with something delicious.
- Discourage chewing inappropriate items by spraying them with chewing deterrents. The first time you use a deterrent, put a dab on a piece of tissue or cotton ball, and put it directly into your Siberian's mouth. Ideally, he'll spit it out. If your dog finds the deterrent really distasteful, he might shake his head, drool, or retch. With luck, he'll make the connection between the taste and the odor of the deterrent, and be more likely to avoid items that smell like it. Spray the deterrent on every object you don't want your dog to chew. Reapply the deterrent every day for two to four weeks. Some commonly used deterrents are Veterinarian's Best Bitter Cherry Spray, Bitter YUCK! No Chew Spray, and plain old Tabasco sauce. Do realize, however, that successfully stopping destructive chewing requires more than just the use of deterrents. Dogs must learn what they can chew as well as what they can't chew.
- Supervise your dog until you feel confident that his chewing behavior is under control. Whenever Tavik chews the wrong thing, take it away and give him something he's allowed to chew. No yelling, no thwacks with a newspaper or fly swatter—just matter-of-fact corrections in a firm, lower-pitched tone of voice. "No, mine; this is yours" would be appropriate.

PERSONALITY POINTERS
Siberian Husky Body Language

Siberian Mood	Friendly	Curious or Excited	Playful
Stance	Relaxed	Advancing; stiff; active, often dancing	Advancing; active, often dancing
Posture	Leaning forward	Leaning forward	Elbows on the ground, rear in the air in play bow
Eyes	Soft	Lit up; pupils may dilate	Partially closed during play bow; open and alert; lit up
Ears	Relaxed	Up and forward	Up and forward
Mouth	Lips loose; open slightly	Closed; open slightly	Wooing or slightly open with faint grin
Tail	Relaxed	Horizontal, may wag stiffly or broadly and slowly	Up and wagging broadly

- When you can't supervise directly, you must prevent him from inappropriate chewing. If you work during the day, use a crate, put him in his outside kennel, or, as a truly last resort, put your dog in a small room with the door closed. Remove everything that your dog shouldn't chew from his confinement area, and give him a variety of appropriate toys and chew items to enjoy instead.
- Provide your dog with plenty of physical exercise and mental stimulation. If you have to leave your dog alone for more than a short period of time, make sure he gets out for a good play session beforehand.

DO NOT . . .
- hit, scold, or punish him after the fact. He cannot connect your punishment with something he did hours or even minutes ago.
- use duct tape to hold your dog's mouth closed around a chewed object. This will teach your dog nothing, and can be fatal.
- tie a damaged object to your dog. This will teach your dog nothing.
- muzzle your dog to prevent chewing.

Apprehensive or Anxious	Fearful	Submissive
Retreating, lowered; tense	Retreating, lowered; tense	Retreating, lowered, head turned away
Body and head lowered; may roach back	Elbows and knees bent in crouch, back hunched	Lowered; groveling; may roll over and lift rear leg
Darting	Dilated pupils, eyes narrowed and turned away	Turned away; may squint
Wide	Pinned back	Back and down
Open, showing tongue; panting	Panting, all teeth showing; may lick the air	Lips open to show front teeth; nudge other with muzzle; attempt to lick mouth or hand of other
Stiff or tucked; may wag tip	Tucked tight; may flick tip	Tucked; may flick tip

Escaping

Every dog behaves according to his genetic makeup, which can be presumed from his ancestry. For the Siberian, that means sled dog and that means running. Certainly not all, but some Siberians, will go to great lengths for an opportunity to satisfy their need for exercise and their inherent curiosity. A loose Siberian is in harm's way, and as a responsible owner, you need to do all you can to keep your Siberian safely at home.

Know that you will not be able to train your Siberian to recognize or respect boundaries. The size of your yard is not a natural barrier or deterrent to a dog that is bred to run long distances at a moderate speed without tiring. If he wants to go badly enough, the Siberian will endure the momentary zap an electronic containment system (invisible fence) can deliver. A real fence and supervision is necessary.

Prevention is key. At minimum, you need a sturdy, 6-foot (1.8-m) fence. If you're building a new fence, bury the fencing fabric at least 18 inches (45 cm) into the ground vertically; to retrofit an existing fence, bury woven wire, welded wire, or galvanized mesh horizontally at the base of the fence, extending at least 2 feet (60 cm) into the yard. This will prevent your Siberian from digging under the fence. Make sure there are no gaps where fence meets building—Siberians can squeeze through the tiniest openings. If the fence has an exterior gate, lock it with a brass padlock; brass doesn't rust. Keep the key inside your house. Siberians are quite capable of flipping up an unlocked chain-link gate latch. Slide-and-hook-over latches stump dogs but don't prevent humans from leaving the gate open, so a lock is best. Keep everything he can climb up on, such as doghouses, ladders, and wheelbarrows, away from the fence. Ideally, before your Siberian escapes, you can teach him to stay away from the fence:

- Don't allow your dog in the yard unsupervised until he has been trained to stay away from the fence.
- Attach a 15–20-foot (4.5–6-m) length of high-test fishing line to your Siberian's collar and allow him to drag the line around in the yard for a few minutes every day, until he no longer pays any attention to it.
- When you're ready and he's not paying any attention to you or the line, attach a strong dowel to the loose end, and then have a helper appear on the other side of the fence.
- The second your Siberian puts his feet on the fence, yank him backward firmly, drop the line, and turn away. If he's a puppy or young dog, you won't need to pull very hard. If he's an adolescent or adult, you'll need to pull with more force.
- Repeat every day until your Siberian will walk up to the fence but not put his feet on it, even with enticements.
- Watch your dog from a distance to make sure he's not putting his feet on the fence when you aren't around. If he is, call your helper and arrange additional training sessions. Ideally, you do not want the dog to associate being pulled off his feet with you. Rather, you want him to associate it with the fence: "When my feet touch the fence, the fence throws me backward."

Should all your efforts to contain your Siberian in the yard fail, you can build him a concrete kennel run inside the fenced yard. Why inside a fenced yard? A fence serves two purposes. One, it keeps trespassers, both human and canine, out of your yard and away from your dog's kennel. And two, a fenced yard provides a safe place for you and your dog to play together. A nice-sized kennel for an adult Siberian should be at least 6 feet tall, 8 feet wide, and 12 feet long (1.8 m tall, 2.4 m wide, and 3.6 m long). Nine-gauge galvanized or aluminized chain-link is the most durable. A step-over gate slows down his exit from the kennel. A concrete floor makes for easy cleaning, and is impossible to dig through. Welded wire, tightly attached to all four top rails, not the chain-link fabric, will prevent him from climbing out. Shade is a must if your Siberian will be spending the day in his kennel. UV-resistant, high-density polyethylene and/or polypropylene screening, such as that used for tennis or baseball windscreens, provides shade and allows ventilation. A heavy-duty rubber bucket, attached to the kennel fence with a double-end

snap, can't be knocked over. A doghouse, preferably with a flat top he can stretch out on, should be placed at the end opposite the kennel door.

Bolting through an open door is another way the opportunistic Siberian escapes. In a perfect world, all the exterior doors in your house open inward, allowing you to block his escape route with your legs. But realistically, all doors do not open inward, and all doors are not opened by adults. In fact, Siberians have been known to open doors themselves. Front doors are particularly dangerous because they usually open to an unfenced yard. An entryway with exterior and interior doors is ideal; baby gating the foyer is also effective. Garage doors need to be kept closed if an interior door opens into the garage. Again, prevention is key. You'll need to prevent your Siberian from storming the door:

- Until you can train him to stay away from the door, put your Siberian in his crate or shut him in another room while you open the door.
- Teach your Siberian to sit and stay on command, and put him in a *sit-stay* well away from the door when you need to open it.
- If your children are old enough and your Siberian will obey them, teach your children to put the dog in a *sit-stay* away from the door before they go to open it. If your children are young, teach them to get an adult to handle the dog and the door.
- If your Siberian is adept at opening doors, keep them locked, install baby-proof doorknobs, hooks-and-eyes, and anything else necessary to keep him from opening them.

It sounds complicated and not much fun, but really, once the escape-proofing is done and you're used to watching doors and gates, it just becomes second nature.

BE PREPARED! Misunderstanding Dominance Theory

The scruff shake and alpha roll methods of asserting dominance over one's dog appeared in dog training literature through the 1950s and was based on wolf research that is now regarded as quite shallow in its interpretations of behavior. Fact is, there is absolutely no scientific evidence that these methods are useful dog-training techniques, but there is plenty of evidence that they can frighten your Siberian and the dog will learn only to fear.

Dominant dogs and wolves do not forcibly roll submissive dogs over onto their backs. Submissive dogs and wolves roll themselves over and expose their bellies as an act of submission. Rather than being forcibly bowled over, the originally observed alpha roll was actually a submissive wolf offering his or her belly. Trying to grapple an already agitated adult Siberian to the ground and roll him over will likely result in injury.

Scruff shakes are used by wolves and dogs to communicate or to kill prey. Tactile communication in wolves is a relatively unexplored area of research, so no one knows what exactly a wolf may be communicating when she grabs her pups by the scruff and gives them a light shake. Siberian mothers rarely, if ever, shake their puppies by the scruff. Other scruff-grabbing and shaking behaviors are clearly intended to break the neck of the prey. Shaking a puppy by the scruff of the neck will most likely injure him. Doing that to a dog the size of an adult Siberian is unlikely to elicit more than a puzzled look.

Guarding/Object Possession

Any dog that aggressively guards his food or toys is dangerous around children. The ideal time to address guarding behavior is in puppyhood. Still, with patience and persistence, you can extinguish guarding tendencies in the older Siberian in your home. Know that you cannot teach your Siberian to allow you to take away his food or toy by repeatedly taking away his food or toy. Doing this simply teaches your dog that his food or toy is in danger. Instead, you have to convince him that you are not a threat. In fact, you are a purveyor of good things.

- Put your dog's bowl down with nothing in it. He'll look at you quizzically, then beg you to fill it.
- Hand-feed your dog. Eventually you'll be able to put your hand in his bowl while he's eating.
- Stand at a distance your dog is comfortable with, and then gradually reduce the distance over time. Drop a few treats into his bowl as you slowly get closer.
- Keep a few pieces of his meal. When he's done and looks up at you, drop the remaining pieces one at a time into the bowl.
- As he is eating, drop a few favorite treats into his bowl.
- Pet and talk to your dog in a calming tone while he's eating. All you're doing at this point is showing your dog that it is a good thing for you to be around.

To combat object possession in your Siberian, first remove everything he guards, including toys, bones, and dog beds. If he guards his spot on furniture or under the coffee table, block his access to the room or keep him leashed and away from those areas. Absolutely everything will be doled out by you until the guarding behavior has been extinguished. Teach your Siberian to trade by selecting a toy he likes but is not wild about, and a handful of treats he likes but doesn't drool over. Give your Siberian the toy. As you reach for the toy with one hand, hold out the treat with the other and say, in a higher-pitched, cheery tone, "Trade!" As soon as he lets go of the toy, praise and treat. Repeat until he almost anticipates the treat by dropping the toy, and understands that whenever you walk by, you might take whatever he has but might replace it with something better.

Siberians are pack-oriented dogs who look to the pack leader for direction. You are the pack leader, and your Siberian should look to you. If your Siberian challenges your authority through growling or showing his teeth, ignore him for several days. Don't pet him when he asks. Make him earn your attention by obeying. Make him sit and hand-feed him. Never overlook or make excuses for a dog's challenge to your authority. Dogs that bite can cause serious injury, leave their owners open to lawsuits, and put themselves in a position to be euthanized. A Siberian that bites cannot be tolerated. Consult a veterinary behaviorist if your Siberian shows signs of aggression toward people.

Communicating with Your Siberian

Scent Smell is a dog's dominant sense, and Siberians live through their noses. They can track another dog team that's eight hours ahead, in –20°F (–29°C) weather, on a trail covered with new snow. They can smell open water and the north wind that signals fall's arrival, and they can smell your dinner coming out of the oven, even when they're upwind. Siberians meet and greet other dogs and, unfortunately, some people, by sniffing genitals, anuses, faces, and ears, and they learn quite a bit about other dogs or people this way. Your Siberian's behavior is often influenced by his sense of smell. He can smell your stress, so he stays away. Research suggests he can smell the difference between tears of joy and anger, and acts accordingly. Your dog remembers all the scents he's ever identified, all the people and dogs he's ever met. People, on the other hand, don't use smell to communicate much at all.

Voice Siberians, like their wolf counterparts, communicate with their voices. They howl, yelp, trill, woo-woo, yowl, yodel, growl, shriek, roar, and occasionally woof. Based on the context of these vocalizations, you'll learn to understand what your Siberian is telling you. Your dog, on the other hand, has only your tone of voice to help him figure out what you're saying. Speaking louder and louder and saying the same thing over and over will not cure your Siberian of selective deafness. Dogs have an incredible sense of hearing, so volume is rarely necessary to get your Siberian's attention. If you want to play with, encourage, or excite your Siberian, speak to him in a higher pitch. When you want your Siberian's rapt attention during training or competition, for example, you'll need your best command voice. A firm, matter-of-fact, short command delivered at a lower pitch signals you mean what you're saying, and since Siberians are capable of detecting even the slightest change in timbre, he'll respond to the leadership in your voice. And when he does, don't forget the calm, positive praise in a higher pitch.

Facial Expressions Siberians have the most expressive faces of any breed. Their eyebrows can signal confusion, amazement, determination, and disgust; their eyes, affection, pain, and intense interest. When they're happy, their eyes light up and they smile; if they aren't sure, they cock their heads, pull their ears up high, and raise their eyebrows, waiting for you to explain further. They squint their eyes and pull their ears back when they're suspicious. When they're stalking a squirrel, their expression is one of intense concentration—eyes focused like lasers on their prey, ears forward, brow furrowed, mouth closed with lips drawn back just a little. And they can read your facial expressions just as easily as you can read theirs because they watch your every move and know your behavior patterns. Your Siberian knows that a smile means you're pleased with him and a scowl means you're not. He's so good at detecting movement, he can pick up even subtle changes in your face. Your expression, your tone of voice, and your body posture tell your Siberian all he needs to know.

Body Posture

Siberians use their bodies when they interact with other dogs and people to signal their intentions, to instigate play, and to express their emotions. An excited Siberian's tail can whirl like a propeller; a playful Siberian will bow and grin, tail wagging furiously, then leap sideways into the air and dash away, inviting a chase. Your confident, well-socialized Siberian will walk down the street with an easy gait, his head held high, ears up, with a relaxed, gently wagging tail. If he's not feeling well or is in pain, he'll tell you with squinting eyes, ears wide on a head held low, and perhaps an arched back. Your Siberian can interpret your body postures as friendly, challenging, or dominating, depending on the circumstances and his experiences. Siberians are more likely to come when you call them if you crouch down and open your arms in a welcoming gesture than if you're standing straight and tall. But if you crouch down and call your Siberian with a frown on your face, a stern look in your eye, and a happy tone of voice…well, he'll rightly be confused and a little suspicious.

Vision

Siberians have up to a 290-degree field of vision and are able to see in the dark and in dim light four times better than humans, but their visual acuity is somewhat less. What you can see with sharp clarity at 75 feet (22.5 m) looks blurry to your dog at 20 feet (6 m). And that's OK, because a dog's ability to detect movement and decipher what that movement signifies is more important. Your movements and gestures give him important clues about what will happen next. You look at the leash hanging on the wall, he runs to the door ready to go for a walk; you point, he follows your finger. Sometimes, though, the body postures and behaviors humans use in interactions with dogs are misread, although not because the dog didn't see them clearly. Teach your dog your own body posture signs and make a point of getting to know his. By observing your Siberian's reactions to you and others, you can avoid sending confusing signals in any light.

Chapter Six

Health and Nutrition

As a conscientious dog owner, you're responsible for your Siberian's well-being. You feed him nutritious food, you keep him safe and secure, and you provide the mental stimulation and physical exercise he needs to live the full and, typically, long life every Siberian deserves. Add to your list of responsibilities choosing a veterinarian.

Choosing a Veterinarian

Your Siberian's veterinarian is the second-most important human in his life when it comes to his health, so it stands to reason that you will want to make a careful and informed choice. The breeder of your Siberian, your dog-owning friends, and the American Animal Hospital Association's locating service are good sources for finding skilled doctors, but you will also want to physically go to the clinics, without your dog, to personally interview all prospective choices. Remember that the veterinarian you choose will be partnering with you to provide health care for your Siberian for perhaps 15 years or more.

Proximity, available services, and cost should be secondary to selecting a veterinarian who has a lot of experience with Siberian Huskies, readily communicates with you, and interacts well with your dog. When you've narrowed your list, interview each veterinarian personally. If the veterinarian can answer your questions in an informative, helpful way, you may have made a good choice. But don't be afraid to take your dog to another veterinarian if you're not happy when you take your dog in for his first visit; it might take a couple of tries to find a veterinarian who works well with you and your dog, but once you find that perfect one, you'll know.

Your Siberian's First Checkup

Your puppy's first visit to his new veterinarian should not be scheduled until it's time for his next puppy shot, unless he becomes ill or your contract says otherwise. Most older dogs, rescue, and shelter dogs have already been heartworm tested, put on preventive, spayed or neutered, vaccinated,

BE PREPARED! Visiting and Interviewing a Potential Veterinarian

You can learn a lot about a veterinary clinic in a single visit by observing closely, listening carefully, and asking questions.

- Do the animals visiting the clinic appear to like the staff and the doctor(s)?
- Do the staff and veterinarian(s) appear to enjoy their clients and their work?
- How do the veterinarian(s) and staff interact with the owners?
- Does the facility look and smell clean?

Include the following on your list of questions to ask:

- How much and what kind of experience does the veterinarian have with Siberian Huskies?
- How does the veterinarian keep up with the latest research and best practices?
- What types of surgeries is the veterinarian qualified to perform?
- How does the clinic handle emergencies?
- Does the clinic have relationships with specialists?
- Does the clinic offer wellness packages?
- What types of alternative medicine does the clinic offer?

and microchipped before being placed. To avoid unnecessary procedures make sure to take your dog's vaccination and worming record with you. Typically, the veterinarian will check your Siberian from head to toe, listen to his heart and lungs, and palpate his abdomen. You will also want a stool sample checked for worms and their eggs. If your Siberian is an older puppy or adult, have blood drawn for a heartworm check before starting him on heartworm preventive.

When it comes time to discuss vaccinations, remember that not all dogs should be vaccinated annually for everything just because the shots are available! Your locale and travel plans, your dog's access to other animals and wildlife, his age, and anything else that may affect his risk of exposure to disease should be part of the discussion you and your veterinarian will have about your Siberian's vaccination schedule going forward. Remember, more is not necessarily better when it comes to vaccines—there are many successful vaccination schedules.

If mosquitoes live where you and your dog live or travel, you also need to talk with your veterinarian about heartworm preventive medication. Preventive products should be used year-round, even in areas where mosquitoes occur only seasonally. Dogs over six months of age should be checked for heartworm infection before preventive medication is started to avoid adverse reactions in those with preexisting heartworm infection. Prevention is safe, convenient, and effective, and much cheaper and safer than treating heartworm infection.

Common Health Concerns

Siberians are energetic, inquisitive, spirited dogs whose inclinations may leave them vulnerable to certain upsets and mishaps. It's up to you to recognize the hazards, mitigate them when you can, and know what to do when they happen. If you are not familiar with basic first aid, check with your veterinarian, local dog training club, or local Red Cross chapter for a class in your area. A basic first aid kit for dogs should include the following items:

> Ace bandage/vet wrap in varying widths
> Telfa pads (nonstick bandage)
> Triple antibiotic ointment
> KY Jelly (for taking temperature)
> Rectal thermometer
> Cotton balls
> Cotton swabs
> Alcohol (isopropyl)
> Hydrogen peroxide
> Betadine (iodine-based antiseptic)
> Sterile gauze pads
> Splint material (rolled magazine, stick, dowel)
> Karo syrup
> Muzzle (old pantyhose work well)

Like any other dog, your Siberian will most likely catch a minor illness or two at some point in his life. Because you regularly monitor your dog's condition and know what's normal for him, you can quickly notice when something isn't right. Check him over to decide if a trip to the veterinarian is warranted.

Diarrhea Although many Siberians have cast-iron stomachs, others have sensitive digestive systems, and the least little change in diet or water source, or getting into the garbage—a.k.a. dietary indiscretion—will cause a mild case of diarrhea. The best treatment for mild diarrhea in the adult Siberian is to withhold food for 24 hours, provide only small amounts of water every few hours, and then give several small meals of cooked rice and hamburger meat. However, diarrhea can also be caused by intestinal

CAUTION

Leptospirosis Vaccines

Siberians are known to have adverse reactions to leptospirosis vaccines, especially including swelling of the face and mucous membranes. Vaccination does not fully protect your Siberian, because currently available vaccines contain only two to four of the fifteen or more pathogenic leptospirosis strains and do not offer cross protection against strains not contained in the vaccine. Find out which strains are prevalent in your area and what the incidence rates are for lepto in dogs in your area. If the incidence rates are high, your Siberian is highly likely to be exposed to standing water that is contaminated with the urine of infected dogs and/or wildlife, and if the prevalent strains in your area are available in a vaccine, then consider vaccinating your dog **twice** a year using individual, not combination, shots. Because of the lack of cross protection between strains, the high incidence of reactions, and the need for **twice-yearly** inoculation, many veterinarians have begun to recommend leptospirosis vaccinations only for those dogs at high risk.

FYI: Heartworm Life Cycle

- Mosquito feeds on infected mammal, ingesting larval heartworms called microfilaria. The American Heartworm Society says heartworm disease has become a worldwide clinical concern affecting more than 30 species. An estimated 1 million dogs in the United States are infected. There are more than 60 different species of mosquitoes that can transmit heartworms.
- Microfilaria mature in 10 to 14 days and move to mosquito's mouthparts.
- Mosquito bites an uninfected dog, injecting heartworm larvae into the dog's skin.
- Heartworm larvae burrow until they penetrate blood vessels. Blood carries them to the heart, lungs, and associated blood vessels, where larvae mature. Initially the worms cause inflammation of the vessels, then enlargement of the heart, congestive heart failure, and death. An adult female heartworm measures up to 1 foot (30 cm) long and can live five to seven years. A single dog can harbor as many as 250 heartworms.
- Adult heartworms mate and produce microfilaria that circulate in the dog's blood vessels, waiting to be sucked up by the next mosquito that flies by. The entire cycle typically takes six to seven months, but can take up to ten months.

parasites, obstruction, poisoning, and many diseases. Persistent diarrhea, with or without blood, accompanied by vomiting and/or fever, can indicate a serious problem. Dehydration is a major concern, especially in young and old dogs. Contact your veterinarian as soon as possible and **before** administering human medications.

Insect Bites and Stings Siberians are active, outdoorsy types. They chase and snap at bees and wasps, they love to dig, and they will charge into the underbrush when given the chance. These behaviors leave them vulnerable to insect bites and stings. Typically, the dog doesn't even notice he's been bitten and veterinary care is unnecessary, but occasionally Siberians do have more severe allergic reactions. The most common symptoms associated with an insect bite reaction include a swollen face or muzzle, difficulty breathing, vomiting or diarrhea, and restlessness. Some dogs will progress to severe respiratory distress and anaphylactic shock. This is a severe allergic reaction or acute hypersensitivity reaction and is often recognized by sudden collapse and severe breathing difficulties. You should seek veterinary care immediately if you think your Siberian may be experiencing anaphylaxis.

Hyperthermia Your Siberian will enjoy playing, running, and hiking with you. Running is in his DNA, and he may not know when to quit, so it's up to you to prevent his overheating. Sled dog drivers use the 120 rule: If the combined total of temperature plus humidity equals more than 120 (110 if it's sunny and humid), don't allow the dog to exercise strenuously. It is important to remember that dogs do not regulate their body temperature by sweating as humans do—they cool themselves by panting.

If you intend to bike or run in the summer with your Siberian, plan to take lots of water breaks in the shade or leave your dog at home. Watch for lethargy, disorientation and uncoordinated movements, profuse and rapid panting, thick drooling saliva, wide eyes with a glassy look, and/or vomiting and diarrhea. Look at his tongue—a brick red, foot-long (30 cm) tongue signals overheating.

Should the unthinkable happen, a controlled reduction of your dog's body temperature is the priority. Spray him with **tepid** water, if available, to the skin and put him in front of a fan. Massaging his legs will move stagnant air and help dissipate heat. Rubbing alcohol can be applied to his footpads to dilate pores and increase perspiration. Closely monitor his rectal temperature and stop the cooling treatment immediately when his temperature has dropped to 103°F (39.7°C) to avoid the equally serious problem of hypothermia. A Siberian's normal temperature is

Helpful Hints

Pet Insurance

Health insurance for dogs is available through several different companies. Premiums cost between $10 and $90 per month, depending on the deductible, the breed and age of your dog, and where you live. The list of exclusions is long, and some insurers will exclude your dog's condition from coverage at renewal. Most have per illness, yearly, and lifetime payout caps. An alternative to insurance is to budget for routine costs and add several hundred dollars each year to an emergency savings fund for your Siberian's care.

CHECKLIST

Routine Health Check

Schedule a day, perhaps his monthly heartworm medication day, to go over your dog. Make copies and use this checklist to note anything out of the ordinary. Date it so you have a record.

Weight: ☐ Unchanged   ☐ Increase   ☐ Decrease

Mouth: ☐ Bad breath   ☐ Masses   ☐ Tartar buildup   ☐ Loose teeth
            ☐ Dead teeth   ☐ Blood

Gum Color: ☐ Pink (correct)   ☐ Splotchy   ☐ Pale   ☐ Blue
            ☐ Bright red

Gums: ☐ Growths   ☐ Bleeding   ☐ Swelling   ☐ Lesions

Nose: ☐ Cool and moist (correct)   ☐ Discharge   ☐ Sores
            ☐ Dry   ☐ Hot to the touch

Eyeballs: ☐ Swollen   ☐ Unequal pupils   ☐ Visible scratch/cut
            ☐ Red conjunctiva/yellow sclera   ☐ Glassy or dull surface

Eye Rims: ☐ Tearing   ☐ Redness   ☐ Squinting   ☐ Discharge
            ☐ Pawing at eyes

Ears: ☐ Bad smell   ☐ Redness   ☐ Fly strikes
            ☐ Pawing/scratching at ear   ☐ Head-shaking/tilting
            ☐ Holding ear at odd angle   ☐ Debris in ear

Legs: ☐ Limping   ☐ Lumps   ☐ Swelling at joint

Feet: ☐ Swelling   ☐ Fissure in webbing   ☐ Pad cuts/splits
            ☐ Torn nails

Skin and Coat: ☐ Flea dirt   ☐ Tick   ☐ Hair loss   ☐ Hot spot
            ☐ Bad smell   ☐ Greasy   ☐ Lump   ☐ Scabs

Abdomen: ☐ Distended   ☐ Painful   ☐ Noisy

Heart Rate: (Normal is 80–120 bpm, depending on weight)
            ☐ Racing   ☐ Too slow

Genitals: ☐ Discharge   ☐ Swelling   ☐ Bloody urine

Anal Region: ☐ Swelling   ☐ Licking rear   ☐ Scooting rear   ☐ Redness
            ☐ Worms in stool or around anus   ☐ Bloody or black diarrhea

Tail: ☐ Swollen   ☐ Unmoving   ☐ Kinked

between 100.5°F and 101.5°F (38–39°C), but again, you want to stop the cooling treatment immediately when his temperature has dropped to 103°F (39.7°C) to avoid hypothermia.

Hereditary Disorders

All living things, including humans and all breeds of dogs, have the potential to produce hereditary disorders. Siberian Huskies are fortunate in that the breed is generally healthy, with few breed-related genetic issues. Incidence rates for these disorders have always been very low and continue to drop, primarily because of the vigilance of ethical breeders who follow breeding program guidelines established by geneticists and take advantage of rapidly advancing research and available genetic screening programs.

Hip Dysplasia

Hip dysplasia literally means an abnormality in the development of the hip joint. It is characterized by a shallow acetabulum (the socket of the hip joint) and changes in the shape of the femoral head and neck (the "ball" of the hip joint). Severe arthritis can develop as a result of the malformation of the hip joint and can result in pain as the disease progresses. Hip dysplasia is a polygenetic inherited condition, but not all dogs with the genetic tendency will develop clinical signs. Dogs with no genetic predisposition do not develop hip dysplasia. See the Orthopedic Foundation for Animals' website for the dysplasia statistics for Siberians and most other breeds, including numbers of animals evaluated, hip ratings, and prevalence rankings among breeds. If you decide to purchase a puppy and choose a breeder carefully, you are not likely to have a Siberian with hip dysplasia.

Hereditary Eye Disorders

Only three of the myriad eye problems known in dogs are found with any frequency in the Siberian Husky: bilateral cataracts (juvenile cataracts), crystalline corneal opacities (corneal dystrophy), and progressive retinal atrophy (PRA). Each disorder presents in a different portion of the eye; eye color is not a factor in inheritance.

Bilateral Cataracts in the Siberian are thought to be the result of a recessive gene, thus allowing unaffected dogs to be carriers. The cataracts can appear as early as three months of age and as late as eighteen months. Progression is slow, and severity ranges from mild to total blindness. Geneticists are developing a DNA test to detect carriers of the gene, and affected dogs are not used for breeding.

Crystalline Corneal Opacities (Corneal Dystrophy) occur when cholesterol is abnormally deposited in the cornea, the outer transparent portion of the eyeball. Vision is seldom affected and the disorder is not painful. Siberians have a form properly called "crystalloid corneal dystrophy," which is inherited as a recessive trait. This form of dystrophy usually appears between five and twenty-seven months as a white, round or oval haze

Breed Truths

Eye Color

Those exotic Siberian eyes come in many colors and combinations of colors, and NONE of those colors or combinations are associated with any sort of genetic defect. The eyes can be blue, or shades of brown from very dark to light, including hazel and amber. Combinations include one blue and one brown eye, a brown eye with a blue spot or wedge and vice versa, or a half-brown, half-blue eye. The mode of inheritance for eye color in Siberians is unknown, but appears to be independent of coat color or markings.

in the center of the cornea, occasionally as a doughnut-shaped opacity in the peripheral cornea. There is no cure for corneal dystrophy, but neither is there usually a need for treatment.

X-Linked Progressive Retinal Atrophy is a degenerative disease of the retina. As the dog loses his ability to see in low light, dilation of the pupils and the reflection of light from the back of the eye become more pronounced. In XL-PRA, the defective gene is a recessive trait found on the X chromosome. Females who inherit a defective gene on the X chromosome from one parent and a normal gene on the X from the other won't be affected, but will be carriers. A male puppy with a carrier dam gets either a defective or a normal gene on the X chromosome his dam gives him. And if it's the defective gene, he will be affected. The disease in males is devastating. The good news is that the incidence rate in Siberians is very low, and a DNA test to identify carrier females was made available in 2001, so that X-linked PRA can be eliminated from the breed.

Complete, Balanced, and High Quality Food

Your Siberian will eat just about anything, but his overall health and longevity greatly depends on proper nutrition from puppyhood to old age. Most premium dog foods on the market are the result of decades of research to make sure they meet the minimum complex nutritional requirements of a healthy dog, and are designed to be the dog's sole source of nutrition. Which is best for your Siberian? As long as you feed your dog the correct amount of a high-quality, highly digestible, high-protein, high-fat dog food that he'll eat and that agrees with him, you've made the right choice. Here are some tips for determining digestibility and protein and fat quality.

Digestibility determines the volume of food your dog must eat to meet his nutritional requirements. The more digestible the ingredients, the less volume he must eat to get the nutrition he needs. Dogs have a relatively short digestive tract. This means food passes through quickly—in hours, not days—so vegetables and grains, which are just 40–60 percent digestible, have to be pre-processed for your dog to get any nutrition at all out of them. Additionally, the "crude fiber" amount appearing on the guaranteed analysis list is an estimate of how much of the food is fiber, which is completely indigestible.

Breed Truths

Feeding Methods

Siberians are not good candidates for self-feeding or timed feeding plans because they eat every meal like it may be their last. In other words, most Siberian Huskies will enthusiastically overeat at every opportunity. You are better able to monitor your Siberian's body condition when you control the amount of food available to him at each meal.

Food Bowl Placement

Dogs naturally guard their food, so where you feed your Siberian is more important than when you feed him. To avoid any sort of potentially dangerous situation, make sure you put his bowl down in a place where no other family pet(s) or children have access to it. And, as soon as your dog has emptied his bowl, which usually doesn't take long, pick it up.

Protein Quality refers to the availability of the 10 essential amino acids that the dog must get from food in specific amounts. Complete proteins, such as whole eggs, meat, and fish, contain these 10 essential amino acids in the correct proportions; incomplete protein sources such as soy, corn, and wheat don't, and have to be properly blended with other amino acid sources to come up with the correct balance to meet the dog's needs.

For example, corn has only four of the ten essential amino acids, so when used as an ingredient in dog food, it must be combined with other protein sources that can supply the remaining six essential amino acids not found in corn. The "Balanced" part of the "Complete and Balanced" label on dog food is stat-

FYI: Nutritional Requirements

Siberian Huskies are quite sensitive to nutritional deficiencies. Their coats will get dry, they will start to shed continuously, and their skin will itch MUCH faster than most other breeds. Remember these points when choosing or changing your dog's food:

- He should thrive on a premium, meat-based food that is highly digestible, with a high-protein and high-fat content. Adjust quantity, not quality, to maintain ideal body condition.
- Look at your dog, use common sense, and, based on his age and activity level, feed the amount that will maintain his ideal weight.
- Many Siberians do not tolerate soy well, and most dogs over the age of four months do not tolerate milk products. Cultured dry cottage cheese and yogurt are well tolerated because they contain very little lactose.
- Think twice before feeding your dog a home-cooked or raw diet. Dog food must be formulated to meet your Siberian's nutritional needs. Feeding raw or home-cooked meals requires knowledge and is time consuming and expensive.
- Variety is not the spice of life when it comes to your dog's food. A drastic change to his daily diet can cause stomach upset. Feed only a few treats or a small amount of leftover steak daily.
- If you must change brands of commercial dog food, do it slowly over several weeks. Start by substituting a quarter of the old ration with new food for several days. If your Siberian doesn't develop loose stools, feed half old food and half new for a week, then a quarter old and three-quarters new, and so on.

ing that the minimum required amounts of all 10 essential amino acids are contained in the food. It is not making any claims about the digestibility of the protein sources blended to attain that balance. You can have the world's most perfectly balanced protein, but if the dog can't digest it, it is useless.

Fat is a highly concentrated source of energy for dogs, supplying more than twice the energy of protein or carbohydrate. Fats are a must to transport fat-soluble vitamins into the body. The essential fatty acids, which must be supplied by food, are important for a strong immune system and as antioxidants. Dogs don't develop the fat/cholesterol cardiovascular changes seen in humans, so you want to see poultry and/or beef fat, or fish oil, near the top of the ingredient list.

Vitamins and Minerals

Vitamins are organic substances required by a dog's body in minute amounts for many metabolic processes. Most vitamins cannot be synthesized by the body and need to be supplied in food in sufficient quantities. The fat-soluble vitamins (A, D, E, and K) are absorbed in the same way as dietary fats, and excess amounts are stored primarily in the liver.

BE PREPARED! Dietary Hazards and Poisonous Plants

Siberians will eat just about anything, including dandelion roots, pin cherries, and chocolate. Although the dandelion roots are safe for your Siberian to eat, the pin cherries and chocolate are not. Here are more common poisonous foods, plants, and household chemicals posing a danger to dogs:

Foods

Grapes and Raisins	Contain an unknown toxin that can damage the kidneys and cause death.
Xylitol	The artificial sweetener found in sugar-free gum can cause the blood pressure to drop, leading to liver failure and death.
Chocolate	Contains methylxanthines, which can affect the heart and nervous systems.
Macadamia Nuts	Unknown toxin causes depression, weakness, vomiting, and tremors.
Mushrooms	Both wild and cultivated mushrooms can be toxic, causing central nervous system effects as well as liver, heart, or kidney damage. Clinical signs begin six to eight hours after ingestion.
Fruit Pits	Cyanogenic glycosides result in cyanide poisoning indicated by brick-red mucous membranes, dilated pupils, difficulty breathing, panting, and shock.
Avocados	Leaves, fruit, seeds, and bark of avocado trees contain persin, which can cause vomiting and diarrhea in dogs.

Plants

Cyclamen	Terpenoid saponins cause salivation, vomiting, and diarrhea. After large ingestions of tubers: heart rhythm abnormalities, seizures, and death.
Kalanchoe	Bufadienolides produce gastrointestinal irritation and can seriously affect cardiac rhythm and rate.
Pothos	If chewed or ingested, calcium oxalates can cause significant irritation and swelling of the oral tissues and other parts of the gastrointestinal tract.
Sago Palm	Cycasin causes vomiting and diarrhea, weakness, seizures and liver failure, and death.
Schefflera	Calcium oxalate crystals cause intense burning and irritation of the mouth, lips, and tongue; excessive drooling; vomiting; and difficulty swallowing.

Water-soluble vitamins are generally absorbed in the small intestine, and excess amounts are excreted in the urine. If your dog is eating a well-balanced dog food, vitamin supplementation isn't necessary.

Minerals are critical, inorganic compounds necessary for life. The body cannot manufacture any of them, so getting them in the correct ratios, in food, is vital. Chelated or sequestered forms of minerals are more readily metabolized than minerals commonly supplied in the form of oxides, sulfates, or phosphates. Vitamins and minerals act in concert in the body, so any change to their delicate balance will throw everything off. For example, the correct ratio of calcium to phosphorus and magnesium is very important—excess

Fun Facts

Grass Eating

Eating grass is a common behavior in normal dogs and not associated with illness or nutritional deficiencies. Research at the University of California–Davis also concluded that about 22 percent of grass-eating dogs regularly regurgitate afterward.

BE PREPARED! Other Household Poisons

Human Medications	Over-the-counter and prescription medications, including ibuprofen, painkillers, dietary supplements, and cold medications, represent the number one poisoning hazard to dogs.
Rodenticides	Three different types: 1. Dicoumarol is an anticoagulant. 2. Bromethalin causes tremors, seizure, and paralysis. 3. Cholecalciferol causes blood calcium to rise, triggering acute renal failure.
Antifreeze	Ethylene glycol causes stumbling, vomiting, and depression. Seizures, increased urination, and increased thirst may also be seen. The kidneys are most severely affected, and even if the dog seems to improve initially with treatment, he may succumb to kidney failure three to five days post-ingestion. Success of treatment is dependent upon *quick* treatment. **If you suspect that your dog has come into contact with antifreeze, contact your veterinarian immediately.**
Insecticides/Pesticides Herbicides	Organophosphates (diazinon, malathion) and carbamates (carbaryl, methomyl) can cause chronic anorexia, muscle weakness and twitching, constricted pupils, respiratory failure, fever, vomiting, and diarrhea. Many pest control companies now offer "pet-safe solutions."
Ice Melt	Calcium and sodium chloride are paw irritants that can be poisonous if licked off. Paws should be washed and dried as soon as the animal comes in from the snow.

If you suspect your dog has been poisoned by chemicals, foods, or plants, don't panic. A quick response is important, and panicking won't speed things along. Take a moment to collect any material involved so your veterinarian or the poison control center (888-426-4435) can determine what poison or poisons are involved. Take the material and any vomit or feces with you if you go to the veterinarian. If you see your Siberian eating something you suspect might be toxic, do not hesitate to seek emergency assistance, even if you don't notice any adverse effects. Sometimes your dog may appear normal for several hours or days after the incident.

calcium causes decreased phosphorus absorption; lack of magnesium causes decreased calcium absorption. Iron deficiency results in anemia, but too much iron can cause reduced zinc absorption. Supplementing your dog's high-quality commercial dog food with minerals should never be done without veterinary oversight—the health risks are too great.

Body Condition

Siberians are known for their efficiency—and that includes metabolizing food—so they need less food to maintain an ideal weight than most other breeds their size. Siberians are supposed to be athletic and lean, and their health and longevity depend on maintaining a good weight from puppyhood to old age. You can easily see and feel your dog's body condition.

Siberians should have an obvious tuck-up, or waist, that you can see from the side and behind his ribs when you're looking down on him from above. There should be only a thin fat layer at the base of his tail. You should be able to see the shadows of his ribs rippling beneath his coat as he walks by. Monitor your Siberian's body condition routinely—at least once a month—and adjust his food accordingly:

Helpful Hints

Picky Eaters

A picky Siberian is rare indeed, so the axiom "A healthy dog will not starve himself to death" is pertinent when your Siberian won't eat. A sudden refusal to eat usually means a health problem, so check him over and take his temperature. If he acts like he wants to eat but won't, check his mouth for foreign objects, broken teeth, infected gums, sores, or growths. And if he refuses to eat for more than a few meals, contact your veterinarian.

Emaciated Ribs, lumbar vertebrae, pelvic bones, and all bony prominences evident from a distance. No discernible body fat. Obvious loss of muscle mass.

Very Thin Ribs, lumbar vertebrae, and pelvic bones easily visible. No palpable fat. Some evidence of other bony prominence. Minimal loss of muscle mass.

Thin Ribs easily palpated and may be visible with palpable fat. Tops of lumbar vertebrae visible. Pelvic bones becoming prominent. Obvious waist and abdominal tuck evident.

Underweight Ribs easily palpable, with minimal fat covering. Waist easily noted, viewed from above. Abdomen tucked up when viewed from the side.

Ideal Ribs palpable without excess fat covering. Waist observed behind ribs when viewed from above. Abdomen tucked up when viewed from side.

Overweight Ribs palpable with slight excess fat covering. Waist is discernible viewed from above but is not prominent. Abdominal tuck apparent.

Heavy Ribs palpable with difficulty, heavy fat cover. Noticeable fat deposits over lumbar area and base of tail. Waist absent or barely visible. Abdominal tuck may be absent.

Obese Ribs not palpable under heavy fat cover, or palpable only with significant pressure. Heavy fat deposits over lumbar area and base of tail. Waist absent. No abdominal tuck. Obvious abdominal distention may be present.

Grossly Obese Massive fat deposits over thorax, spine, and base of tail. Waist and abdominal tuck absent. Fat deposits on neck and limbs. Obvious abdominal distention.

Chapter Seven

Training and Activities

A well-behaved Siberian Husky will bring great joy to your life. The better he behaves, the more you can do together and the more likely he is to be welcomed nearly everywhere. And since he really is a dog for all seasons, you want him to be welcomed in all sorts of places. Each of the following activities requires some additional training, conditioning, and/or feeding, and all require your Siberian to be a good citizen.

A Dog You Can Live With

No matter what your plans for your Siberian—jogging companion or competitive sled dog, therapy dog, show dog, or couch potato—you want your Siberian to behave in public and in private. No one can live harmoniously with a dog that knocks down little old ladies and wreaks havoc at the veterinarian's office. Such a dog can't be involved in family outings and may easily become a source of resentment for you, your family, and even your friends and neighbors. On the other hand, with basic obedience training, your Siberian can easily be a happy, relaxed, and confident dog you can take anywhere and that is a pleasure to be around.

There are a variety of obedience training methods, but the vast majority of certified dog trainers employ those that use positive reinforcement rather than force and punishment. The theory behind positive reinforcement—rewarding good behavior makes that behavior more likely to occur in the future—makes for happy, well-trained dogs that enjoy learning. Siberian Huskies are particularly receptive to positive reinforcement because they are so highly motivated by food. One of the most common misconceptions about positive training is that dogs trained by this method will perform only if you have treats in your hand. Not true. When you first teach a command, you give a treat and verbal praise each time. Once your Siberian has mastered the behavior, protocol calls for treats only sporadically. When the behavior becomes generalized—he always walks/trots nicely on a leash—he will work for your praise, and food rewards can be phased out completely. One caveat about positive reinforcement training: Your Siberian must ALWAYS be on a leash or long line when outdoors in an unfenced location. No exceptions.

Breed Needs

Training Equipment

Your Siberian should ALWAYS be on a leash or long line when training outdoors in an unfenced location. You'll need a 1-foot (30 cm) and a 6-foot (1.8 m) nylon or soft leather leash, and a 20-foot (6 m) long line (nylon webbing is easiest to grip), in addition to a well-fitting nylon collar (with only enough room to comfortably slide two fingers between the dog's neck and the collar). If your Siberian is still growing, consider an adjustable collar.

Dogs are smart, and they can be taught to do just about anything, from sniffing out cancer to playing peekaboo. Siberians, as you know, are extremely intelligent. Couple their smarts with their incredible instincts and you have a plethora of activities to enjoy together. So get that basic training under your belt and get out there.

Leash Training

Because your Siberian will NEVER go anywhere without one, teaching him to walk, jog, and run with you on a leash is pretty important. Your other option, once he grows up, is being body-surfed down the sidewalk. Leash training will be your Siberian's introduction to self-discipline, and since you can't teach him any other obedience commands until he is comfortable on leash, start working with him as soon as you can find a collar that won't come off over his head. Before you begin

BE PREPARED! Effective Training Tips

- **Be consistent.** Everyone in the family uses the same word and/or hand signal for the same command every time. If you use *"Come"* one week, *"Come here"* and a finger snap the next, and *"Come here, boy"* and a leg pat the following, you'll confuse your dog.

- **Keep chatter to a minimum.** During training sessions, you are teaching a command word associated with a specific behavior. If you bury that command word in a sentence or paragraph, your dog cannot make the association. Save the conversation for another time.

- **Don't repeat the command.** It's easy to do, but it teaches your Siberian that he doesn't need to respond promptly to the first command.

- **Start simple and gradually make it harder.** Proceed step-by-step and give your Siberian lots of practice getting it right. Start with an easy command in a familiar place with no distractions to make it easy for your dog to succeed. Be patient. Only when your dog is responding reliably should you add distance, duration, and finally, distractions. Stand one step away from your dog, then two steps away; ask for a one-second *stay*, then a two- or three-second *stay*; then add another person to the mix.

- **Wait until your dog has mastered the current behavior before you add a new one.** In other words, don't introduce two brand new commands at the same time.

- **Timing is everything.** The Siberian mind is quick, so praise and reward needs to come instantly after the dog does what you want if he's going to make the connection between the behavior and the reward. If the feedback comes even five seconds after your Siberian has done the right thing, he won't make the association.

- **Don't expect too much too soon.** Expect training to take time. Be patient and never punish your dog for failing to do something he has not fully mastered yet. Every Siberian should be given every opportunity to be successful, so until he begins to sit on his own as soon as he hears *"Sit,"* don't expect him to sit without some guidance.

- **Keep it short and sweet.** Siberians bore easily and do not respond to monotonous repetition. Keep it fun and stop before you and your dog get bored or frustrated. Five or ten minutes is plenty at the start. Nothing says you can't do several mini-training sessions during the day, especially if you're training a puppy.

- **Keep your cool.** Yelling at, hitting, or jerking your dog around by the leash won't teach your Siberian to *sit* or *come*. It will teach him that you're unpredictable and to be feared. Calm and consistent training is the only way to get your Siberian to obey and respect you.

- **Keep practicing.** Don't expect that once your dog has learned something, he's learned it for life. He will forget his new skills without regular practice.

leash training a very young puppy, attach a short leash to his collar and let him drag it around, under supervision, for a few minutes a day over several days.

1. Put a collar on your dog and attach a short, soft leash that you can gather up in your hand. Start with your dog at your left knee. Use your left hand and the leash to keep the dog in position, allowing him to neither surge ahead nor lag behind as you walk slowly forward. If you are training a small puppy, you may need to bend over.

2. Lure your dog forward with a tiny piece of treat and give it to him. Continue luring and giving him small treats every few steps. Adjust your stride and speed to the dog's stride length while keeping him at your left knee with the leash.

3. If he stops or fights against the leash, you stop, but say and do nothing. When he relaxes, continue to walk and lure him with the treat and verbal praise. As long as the leash has some slack, say *"Good boy,"* and keep walking.

4. As he gets better at walking beside you, lengthen the leash and phase out the treats by simply substituting verbal praise. Be consistent, even as you add distractions—when he takes the slack out of the leash by charging ahead after a squirrel or lagging behind to sniff a bush, stop walking instantly. Until he returns to your side, stand still.

Sit

The dog who reliably sits on command is a pleasure to live and play with. The *sit* should be the first command you introduce and is one of the easiest to teach. It is also incredibly useful. Your dog can't jump all over a guest, knock the food bowl out of your hand, or dash out the front door when he's sitting. And once your Siberian has the behavior down cold, he'll most likely use it automatically when he wants something from you. (If you have a show puppy, contact your breeder about teaching the *stand* command as well.) You can teach the *sit* in a variety of ways, but the least confusing follows:

1. Start with the dog in front of you, and the short, soft leash and a small treat in your right hand. If he's a small puppy, you may want to kneel on one knee.

2. Hold the leash straight up with your right hand, **gently** push down on the dog's rump with your left hand, and say *"Sit"* in a clear, matter-of-fact tone. As soon as your Siberian's rear is on the floor, say *"Good"* and give him the treat, but don't let him stand up immediately.
3. Once he starts to bend his knees in response to your *"Sit"* command, you can gradually omit **gently** pushing his rump down. When he puts his rump on the floor in response to *"Sit,"* you can gradually omit holding the leash straight up. Reward every positive response with praise and a treat.
4. Continue to practice on leash until he sits every time you tell him to. Only then will you practice the *sit* command off leash in a secure location.

Down

The *down* command is indispensable for living with a Siberian. When you want your dog to be in the room but not in your lap or pacing at the window, or when you want him to rest in the shade during a jogging break, the *down* command is your friend. As soon as your dog will sit despite distractions, get started with the *down* command.

1. Place your dog in a *sit* on your left side and kneel next to him.
2. Say *"Down"* first, then immediately and **gently** pull your dog's head down with the short leash. At the same time, guide him by pressing down between his shoulder blades with the palm of your hand.
3. As soon as his elbows or chest touches the floor, give him a treat and praise, but don't let him get up immediately.
4. After a lot of repetition your Siberian will respond to your verbal command only. When he can respond quickly and reliably, gradually withdraw the treat, but keep the verbal praise.

5. Once he has mastered the *down* from a *sit*, teach him the *down* from a standing position.

Stay

Training any dog to *stay* can be difficult at first because it goes against his natural instinct to be close to his pack, so keep the *stay* command very simple at first and build upon your dog's successes slowly. Once your Siberian can hold a reliable *stay*, you'll find it very useful. It's a great command to use when guests come to your house or if you have problems with your Siberian bolting out the front door. After your Siberian has mastered the *sit*, you can begin to teach the *stay* command.

1. Attach the short leash to your dog's collar, put him in a *sit*, and stand directly in front of him. After one or two seconds, if your dog is still in the *sit*, give him a treat and calm praise. You are rewarding the behavior you want, which is a *stay*, even if it is for only one or two seconds.
2. Begin the process again from the start, this time for three to five seconds. If your dog breaks out of the *stay* at any time, don't give the treat or praise, but simply start the process again for two to three seconds.
3. Now add the hand signal and verbal command "*Stay*" to Step 1. Put your dog in a *sit* and stand directly in front of him. Say "*Stay*" and at the same time hold your hand out in front of you, with your palm facing your dog's nose. Wait a second or two, then praise and reward. Repeat this step over and over, gradually increasing the time between your *stay* command and your praise and treat.
4. Say "*Stay*" and use your hand signal, then take a step backward without tugging on the leash. Pause for a second, then step back to your dog and praise him. Repeat and gradually increase the distance you step back, using longer leashes. Remember to return to your dog before you reward him. Introduce distractions and new locations after your dog can *sit-stay* reliably for a minute or more.

Helpful Hints

Finding a Training Class

Although you can certainly train your Siberian yourself, an obedience class offers not only socialization for your dog, but training tips and experience for you. Ask your veterinarian, breeder, rescue organization, and pet store for recommended training classes in your area. If your Siberian is a puppy, consider puppy kindergarten classes as soon as he's old enough. Check the AKC's website at *www.akc.org* for nearby dog training clubs, the Association of Pet Dog Trainers at *www.apdt.org*, or the National Association of Dog Obedience Instructors at *www.nadoi.org* for opportunities near you. Observe at least two or three instructors or classes, and ALWAYS talk to the instructor who will be teaching your class—club instructors are volunteers with varying degrees of skill.

Come

The *come* command, also known as the recall, is one of the most important skills you need to teach your Siberian. Not only will an unhesitating recall help you avoid that catch-me-if-you-can game at the dog park, but it may help you catch him if he ever gets loose. Never, ever call your dog to you and then punish him. If you want him for something you know he doesn't like, go get him. And don't walk toward him when you're calling him to you. Every time your Siberian comes to you, even when you didn't call him, make sure he's glad he did.

1. Always practice the *come* command in the house or a fenced yard, where there aren't too many distractions. If you're in the house, go to another room. If you're outside, allow your Siberian to get a short distance from you.
2. With a treat in your hand, squat down, open your arms in a welcoming gesture, wave the treat and say, *"Come!"* in an enthusiastic, happy tone of voice.

3. As soon as your dog starts moving in your direction, praise and encourage him with a warm, positive *"Gooood dog!"* If he stops, or starts going away from you, immediately stop the praise. Call his name, ask him again to *"Come,"* and start jogging backward, away from the dog. Clapping your hands may convince him that this is a fun game. When he starts coming toward you again, start the warm praise once more.

4. When your dog makes it all the way to you, give him the treat as well as enthusiastic praise and pets. Then tell your Siberian, *"Go play!"* and let him go back to whatever he was doing for a minute or so.

5. Repeat until your Siberian reliably comes to you every time you call him, then at least once a day for the rest of his life. And every time your Siberian comes to you, make sure he's glad he did.

Leave It

Siberians are enthusiastic and curious about everything, which is why the *leave it* command is such a great tool. If you're out jogging and your dog spots a pigeon, you can tell him to *"Leave it"* rather than planting both feet and hanging on to the leash for dear life until the bird flies away. And when you catch him helping himself to the appetizers on the coffee table, the *leave it* command is perfect. It isn't an easy command to teach, but it's worth it.

1. Use a setting familiar to your dog, that is free of distractions. In one hand you'll have an ordinary *leave it* treat (kibble or other plain treat), and in the other, your dog's very favorite treat—a piece of liver, hot dog, or cheese. Sit down in front of him.

2. Put the ordinary *leave it* treat in your open palm and extend your hand to your dog. Don't say anything. When your dog reaches for the treat, quickly close your hand—don't let him have it. If he then acts uninterested, immediately say *"Yes!"* and give him the special treat from your other hand. If he's really determined to get at the ordinary treat in your closed fist, just hold it out of his reach and ignore him.

3. Wait 10 seconds and do Step 2 again. This time, if he doesn't lunge for the *leave it* treat, enthusiastically say *"Yes!,"* give the special treat from your other hand, and praise and pet. If he goes straight for the ordinary *leave it* treat, close your fist again. He'll most likely look perplexed, and that's OK. As soon as his attention is off the ordinary treat, say *"Yes!,"* give the special treat, and praise and pet.

4. Repeat Steps 2 and 3 many times. Pretty soon your dog will realize that if he doesn't go for the ordinary *leave it* treat, he will be rewarded with a very special treat from the other hand—Siberians are smart!

5. Now that your dog understands the basic behavior it's time to add the verbal *"Leave it."* Continue practicing exactly as you have been all along and say *"Leave it"* just as you start to extend your hand with the ordinary treat in it.

6. Once your Siberian can reliably *leave* the ordinary treat alone, begin to introduce, one at a time, the new twists listed below. Don't proceed too quickly for your dog—take it slow:

- While practicing the *leave it* command hold your hand in different positions—close to the ground or up at your dog's eye level.
- Delay the *"Yes!"* and the special treat until your dog actually looks at you.
- Put the ordinary treat on the floor in front of your dog and say, *"Leave it."* If he goes for the treat, quickly cover it with your foot.
- Move your training sessions into other rooms and eventually outside.
- When you're on your daily walk, with your dog on leash, drop some treats on the ground and walk past them.

The Siberian Good Citizen

Once you're confident your Siberian can handle a walk in the park without incident, you might start thinking about broadening his horizons to include the local pet store or outdoor café. How well will your dog's manners stack up against those of other canine clientele? A fun activity to help you find out is the AKC's Canine Good Citizen test. At this test you and your Siberian will demonstrate your responsible dog ownership and his good manners while he earns the Canine Good Citizen (CGC) title. In order to pass the test, dogs must accomplish each of the following tasks, may not behave aggressively toward people or other dogs, and must refrain from eliminating during the test.

Helpful Hints

Locating a CGC Test

Go to the AKC's website at *www. akc.org/events/cgc* to find a scheduled test near you and to learn more about the CGC program.

Test 1: Accepting a friendly stranger demonstrates that the dog will allow a friendly stranger to approach him and speak to his handler in a natural, everyday situation.

Test 2: Sitting politely for petting demonstrates that the dog will allow a friendly stranger to touch him while he's out with his owner.

Test 3: Appearance and grooming demonstrates that the dog welcomes being groomed and examined and will permit someone, such as a groomer or friend of the owner, to do so.

Test 4: Out for a walk (walking on a loose lead) demonstrates that the handler is in control of the dog. There is a right turn, a left turn, and an about-turn with at least one stop in between and another at the end.

Test 5: Walking through a crowd demonstrates that the dog can move about politely in pedestrian traffic and is under control in public. The dog may show some interest in the strangers but does not jump on people in the crowd or strain on the leash.

Test 6: *Sit* and *down* on command and *staying* in place demonstrates that the dog has training, will respond to commands to sit and down, and will remain in the place commanded by the handler. The dog must *sit* AND *down* on command; then the owner chooses the position for leaving the dog on a *stay* on a line 20 feet (6 m) long.

Test 7: Coming when called demonstrates that the dog will come when called from 10 feet (3 m) away. This test is done on leash.

Test 8: Reaction to another dog demonstrates that the dog can behave politely around other dogs. Two handlers and their dogs approach

117

each other from a distance of about 20 feet (6 m), stop, shake hands and exchange pleasantries, and continue on for about 10 feet (3 m).

Test 9: Reaction to distraction demonstrates that the dog is confident when faced with common distracting situations. Two distractions, such as dropping a chair, a jogger running past, or opening an umbrella, are used.

Test 10: Supervised separation demonstrates that a dog can be left with a trusted person, and will maintain training and good manners.

Traveling with Your Siberian

Your Siberian Husky is tailor-made for activity—so much so that his limiting factor will probably be you! There are a couple of things you need to keep in mind, no matter how far you're going or what activity you and your Siberian enjoy together:

Car Travel: Safety first! You buckle up every time you get in the car, but what about your dog? You certainly don't want him flying around inside the car or, worse yet, being ejected from the vehicle, should you be involved in an accident. A doggie seat belt is not the answer: there are no head restraints, your unsupervised Siberian is likely to chew through the straps in a matter of seconds, and unless the tether pins him to the seat, he can move around in the seat, which makes the seat belt useless as a safety device. While riding in a car, the safest place for your dog is in a crate. His travel crate should be secured to the vehicle. To prevent him from being tossed around inside the crate at every turn, the crate should be just large enough for him to sit up with his shoulders, not the top of his head, touching its ceiling. Heavy-duty wire crates offer good ventilation and can be tied down more easily than molded plastic crates. Just in case you can't speak for your Siberian after an accident, put emergency information on the outside of the crate. If your whole family is on vacation, include the name and contact numbers of a person back home who has agreed in advance to handle emergency veterinary expenses. And don't

CAUTION

Parked Cars

Should you need further convincing about how quickly a car can turn into an oven: A 1995 study compared the temperature rise inside an enclosed, dark-colored vehicle with the temperature rise in a light-colored vehicle with the windows partly open. Within 20 minutes, readings in both cars exceeded 125°F (52°C) and reached approximately 140°F (60°C) in 40 minutes. A dog will suffer brain damage at 107°F (42°C) and die at 120°F (49°C). Don't leave your dog unattended in the car, for even a few minutes, once the outside air temperature exceeds 65°F (18°C).

forget proper identification on your dog. A collar ID tag that's riveted to the collar, rather than hanging on an S-hook, is less likely to get lost. Use the word *Reward* instead of your dog's name, and include both your veterinarian's phone number and yours.

Hotel/Motel Manners: More often than not, family vacations will involve at least one overnight at a hotel or motel. Although there are many hotels and motels that allow pets, most have rules you need to be aware of before you make your reservations. For example, the hotel will usually require you to sign an agreement stating you will be financially responsible for any damage caused by your dog and any expenses incurred by the hotel for pet disturbances. Other common requirements may include a nonrefundable pet guest fee (for special cleaning) or a refundable deposit to guard against damages. In addition, it is up to you, the responsible dog

Helpful Hints

Travel Resources

These and many other online sites help you find pet-friendly hotels, motels, rentals, and even bed-and-breakfasts. Most also have information about traveling with your dog by air, sea, and train.

www.petfriendlytravel.com
www.dogfriendly.com
www.petswelcome.com
www.bringfido.com
www.tripswithpets.com
www.pettravel.com
www.petsonthego.com

owner, to keep hotel and motel doors open to all well-behaved owners and their pets by following these simple rules:

- Bring sheets to cover all furniture, including the bed, to keep the dog hair off everything. If your dog is shedding much, keep him in his crate in the room.
- NEVER leave your dog loose in the room. If he damages the room or disturbs other guests by barking or howling, the management will not be happy.
- Keep a supply of poop bags in your car and use them!
- Make sure there is no leftover food in his bowl when you rinse it in the sink—dog food will clog the drain.

Hitting the Road

Before you head out on your next road trip, get your Siberian micro-chipped. Yes, he'll have an ID tag riveted to his collar, but he can't be separated from a microchip. Once your dog has his microchip, you must register it with a national database. The AKC's national database will accept lifetime registrations for all chips. If your Siberian gets lost, the animal control officer, shelter, or veterinary clinic that finds him can scan for the chip's unique ID number and set the reuniting process in motion.

Helpful Hints

Microchipping

Microchips are injected under your dog's skin and the unique number can be read by a scanner. Consult your veterinarian and go online to read more at *www.homeagain.com*, *www.akccar.org*, or *www.avidid.com*.

While you are at your veterinarian's office getting your Siberian a microchip, you might consider getting a copy of your Siberian's rabies certificate, his vaccination record, and a health certificate. Most states require the rabies certificate to be available for inspection, and some require the dog to have been examined by a veterinarian within 10 days, thus the health certificate. And if your Siberian is taking medication, get his prescription refilled so you'll have enough to last the trip plus several extra days.

Then, make sure you've got everything your Siberian will need for the adventure. He'll be traveling in the car in his crate, of course. You'll want his 6-foot (1.8-m) leash, as well as a 20-foot (6-m) long line or a large (long) retractable lead so he can stretch his legs at rest stops. To avoid stomach upset, pack enough of his food to last the entire trip, and as much of his own water as possible. Pack your canine first aid kit and include your Siberian's microchip number and toll-free registration phone number, a recent photo of your dog, his medication, if any, and detailed contact information for your veterinarian. If your entire family is on the trip, include contact information for someone at home who accepts responsibility for veterinary expenses. And don't forget the poop bags!

Breed Needs

Walk That Dog

What do a school, a farmers' market, and an outdoor café that welcomes dogs have in common? They are places where you just do not want your dog to have to relieve himself. So, plan ahead. Before you and your Siberian take off for an evening of music at the local band shell or a late-afternoon surf, make sure your dog does his business at home. If this is not practical or possible, stop at a rest area or gas station where you can walk your dog before you get to the ballpark or friend's house. If you've planned a longer outing during the times when he is likely to need to go, make a habit of carrying a roll of poop bags in your car, backpack, or pocket.

Traveling by Air

Traveling by air with your Siberian requires a little more planning. First and foremost, no matter where you're going or what it costs, plan to take a direct flight. Direct flights limit the number of times your Siberian is loaded and unloaded, guarantees he won't get left at the layover airport, and cuts down on the time he's in his crate. The second-most important thing is air temperature at time of departure and upon arrival at your destination. The U.S. Department of Agriculture does not allow an airline to accept animals when the temperature is forecast to be above 85°F (30°C) at either end of the flight. You shouldn't consider shipping your Siberian if the temperature is above 75°F (24°C). If you're traveling to warm places during the summer, consider overnight flights. There is also a low temperature restriction, which varies with the airline, and some allow veterinary waivers. Get the specifics directly from your airline.

You will definitely need a health certificate (from your state or the USDA, depending on your destination) issued within 10 days of departure. USDA regulations require your Siberian to be able to stand in his crate with his head up in a normal position, so his airline crate will have to be larger than the crate he uses for traveling in the car. Make sure you get specifics from your airline before you buy another crate. Some will allow metal crates, some only rigid plastic, and some won't take certain-sized crates on certain airplanes. USDA-approved rigid plastic crates, such as the PetMate Pro/Sky Kennel, come with "Live Animal" stickers you can write names and phone numbers on, and food and water containers that clip onto the door. Additionally, take cable ties to the airport with you, in case the airline wants the crate door secured.

Helpful Hints

USDA Requirements for Air Travel

The USDA regulates air travel for all animals. You should always get current specific written information directly from the airline you will be flying before you make reservations. In all cases, the USDA requires the following.

Current Health Certificate—signed within 10 days of outbound travel

USDA-Approved Shipping Crate—dog must have room to stand/turn around, sit/lie down in a natural position

Collar with ID Tags—use riveted style tags; do not use a choke collar

Dog Food—taped to the outside of the crate

Containers for Food and Water—must be inside crate but accessible from outside

Certain types of airplanes allow only a limited number of animals in the cargo hold, so you will need to make a reservation for your dog in advance to be sure you and your dog end up on the same flight. You'll also need to allow extra time to check in for the flight, but you can't check your dog in more than two to four hours before departure, so get this detail in advance.

Perhaps the most important thing to know about flying with your Siberian: **DO NOT** sedate him. Sedation lowers your Siberian's blood pressure, making him unable to regulate his own body temperature. Sedation slows the respiratory process. And, if he's too groggy to clear his ears as the pressure changes occur, his eardrums could be damaged.

You'll need to pack your canine first aid kit; his microchip number and the toll-free number for his microchip registration; copies of his USDA health certificate, rabies certificate, and vaccination record; and a recent photo of your Siberian. You'll also want several days' worth of dog food, an extra 6-foot (1.8-m) leash, his long line or long retractable lead, and poop bags.

If you've had to buy another crate, let your Siberian get used to it before the trip. The night before departure, line the bottom of the crate with shredded newspaper, then cover it with a thin crate pad. Walk your dog into the airport on a leash and don't put him in his crate until the very last minute. When you turn your Siberian over to the airline, put his favorite toy (one he cannot chew up!) in the crate with him. Then, when you get to the boarding gate, tell the agent you are going to wait by the window and watch your dog being loaded. When you get seated on the airplane, tell the flight attendant you have a dog on board, and ask him or her to tell the pilot.

Hiking, Biking, and Such

As much as Siberians love to be on the go, anything more than a mile-a-day (1.6 km) walk may require additional conditioning, activity-specific training for you and your dog, and, perhaps, additional equipment. You will also need to become more attentive to your Siberian's physical condition. For example, long-distance jogging, biking, and hiking should be done on

sand, dirt, or grass trails whenever possible, as asphalt or concrete will wear your dog's pads and nails. Pay especially close attention to temperature and humidity levels in the summer months, so he won't overheat. If you're a real fitness buff, you'll need to watch your dog's weight more carefully, and feed him accordingly. And, if you're new to the activity or a novice at working out with a dog, seek advice from a knowledgeable person—in person! Exercising with your Siberian will be fun and rewarding for both of you, and the biggest bonus? Dogs thrive on routine...so if you establish a regular exercise time, you'll never have to self-motivate—your Siberian will beg you to get up and get going.

Jogging/Running

Here's where the leash training really pays off, because a comfortable 2-mile (3.2-km) jog can't happen if your arm is being yanked out of its socket by an unruly dog. To get started, remember that no matter your Siberian's age and fitness level, conditioning should gradually increase in intensity and length. A dog that is pushed too hard will quit or develop injuries. Don't take more than brisk walks until your Siberian is at least six months old. Be extra careful if you're conditioning an older puppy or obese Siberian. Conditioning sessions should fit your dog's personality; some dogs prefer one long training session broken up by play periods, whereas others, especially older puppies, do better with several short sessions during the day. Start your dog out slowly, just like you would if you were new to running. If you gradually increase distance, your dog's pads will toughen up and make him less susceptible to injury. Check your dog's pads before and after a run for tenderness, raw spots, or bleeding, and if you find anything, give him a few days off. Brisk leash walking should be used for warming up and cooling down—for both you and your Siberian. Plan water stops if your run will last more than 25 minutes, and carry a collapsible water dish or teach your dog to drink out of a water bottle. If you run on a road, teach your dog to stay on your left side, so that he is away from traffic and able to trot along in the grass. Once your dog is trained to stay on your left and maintain a pace (not stop abruptly to sniff or lift his leg), you might

CAUTION

Keep Him Leashed!

No Siberian can ever be trusted off leash. His overwhelming desire to run will always prevail over his training. He'll run until he gets tired, and you will never catch him. That very first dash across the road could be his last, but if he makes it across, you may or may not ever see him again. He might come back if he's not lost, injured, or dead. All Siberians, no matter how well trained, should be confined or on leash at all times. Adequate exercise can easily be obtained on leash, in a fenced area, or in harness.

consider using a retractable lead. The retractable lead will allow your dog to get farther off the road when appropriate, but will stay taut and allow you to reel him in when necessary. The ideal retractable lead has a cord strong enough for a Siberian, a length that will give your dog freedom without sacrificing your ability to control him, and a strong locking mechanism. Should you be fortunate enough to have access to a private trail and your Siberian always trots at your side, you might consider using a hands-free leash. This device consists of a padded belt for you, and a short leash attaching the belt to your dog's collar. If you jog/run at night, outfit your Siberian with a reflective vest and leash. You should also contact a jogging/running club in your area that welcomes dogs, for additional conditioning and feeding tips.

Hiking

In the early 1900s, two great naturalists, John Burroughs and John Muir, sat talking about their dogs, and Burroughs opined that a hiking dog is an "ideal companion because he gives you a sense of companionship without disturbing your sense of solitude." If the number of websites devoted to hiking and backpacking with dogs is any indication, there are countless numbers of dog owners today who feel the same way. If hiking is an activity you enjoy, your Siberian is the perfect companion. And he can carry his own water, food, and first aid kit in an ergonomically designed pack. Of course, your dog needs to be properly conditioned for hiking or backpacking, and you need to be familiar with the sport's etiquette.

Puppies under six months old should be taken on short day trips on less strenuous trails and should not carry packs. In fact, you'll want to wait until your Siberian is at least a year old before he carries a pack. A well-conditioned dog can carry up to one-third of his weight in a pack, but start out with about a third of that weight and increase it slowly as your Siberian becomes better conditioned to carrying a load. Your Siberian will need to be trained to the pack, so allow plenty of time for him to get used to it before setting off on a long trek. First put the empty pack on your dog when you take him for walks, then gradually add more weight and lengthen the time he's wearing it on subsequent outings. If your Siberian hasn't yet hiked at all, take him on short trail jaunts with some weight in the pack so he can get used to handling obstacles such as logs and rocks. After every outing, check that the pack is not chafing under his front legs or elbows.

Helpful Hints

Hiking/Backpacking Resources

A Guide to Backpacking with Your Dog by Charlene G. LaBelle

Hiking with Dogs by Linda B. Mullally

www.wolfpacks.com Informative website

Choose a pack that is large enough to carry the proper load. It should allow plenty of ground clearance and let your dog lie down, even when fully loaded. Panniers (the bags on either side of the harness) should permit the dog's elbows to move normally. Straps should be very snug, loose enough only to slide a finger under. In the beginning check strap fit when your dog is standing, sitting, lying down, and after water breaks. Packs that slide a lot are too loose or poorly balanced. Always pack weight evenly. For example, if your dog is carrying water, put it in small containers that you can distribute evenly. Choose a pack with reflective trim for safety and a grab handle on the harness for serious dog control and assistance over obstacles. And what can your Siberian carry in his pack?

- Water. Never let your dog drink from streams or puddles. Giardia, a parasite that lives in water, can cause stomach problems in humans as well as dogs. And if you'll be out long enough to have to treat water, test your purifying method at home to make sure your dog will drink it.
- Food and snacks. Double-bag individual meals. If the trip is long and strenuous, a snack every two hours, such as a doggie energy bar, will be welcomed. Lightweight bowls are available from many sources. Do not leave dog food on the trail.
- Canine first aid kit. Add a fast-acting antidiarrheal medication to your kit after consulting your veterinarian for recommendations and proper dosage. Know dog first aid before you get to the trailhead!
- Poop bags and trowel.

Make sure you contact management personnel in the area you plan to hike to learn their rules about pets. And while you're talking with them, ask if fleas and ticks are a serious health problem in the area. You may want to talk with your veterinarian about an additional repellant for use during your trek, and you will definitely want to check your Siberian for ticks at the end of each day. Remember that a dog's bark in the backcountry is out of place, a dog crashing through the underbrush startles and frightens all animals, and stepping in dog poop disturbs the solitude. "Leave only footprints" applies to dog poop, so be sure to bury or pack out any droppings. No matter how well behaved your Siberian is, always keep him leashed on the trail, and tied up in camp. If you don't like your dog restrained, then don't take him hiking!

Biking

Biking is another enjoyable way for you and your Siberian to spend time together and get some exercise. However, like strenuous hiking, biking is not an activity for puppies. Your dog should be at least a year old before he starts biking, and reliably leash trained. Instead of simply tying your Siberian's leash to the handlebars or, worse yet, holding his leash—both VERY dangerous actions—get a special bike attachment that secures the dog to the bike while allowing you to keep your hands on the handlebars. Refer to the manufacturer's instructions for teaching yourself and your dog how to use the attachment safely.

A cruiser or mountain-style bike with wider tires works best, especially on the grass or dirt trails that are easier on your Siberian's feet than concrete or asphalt roads. Condition your Siberian slowly, gradually increasing the distance you bike by 5 to 10 percent every four to six rides. Monitor your dog's hydration and stop to rest in the shade if it's sunny, but don't walk away from your bike while your dog is still leashed to it. And keep an eye on your Siberian's feet for raw spots or cuts. He'll be trotting faster than if the two of you were just jogging/running, so wear will happen more quickly. His pads will toughen up over time, but products such as Musher's Secret (a safe paw wax) can help condition, protect, and toughen your dog's pads.

Competitive Dog Sports

Don't worry if you're not exactly the outdoorsy type. There are many other activities you and your Siberian can participate in, especially if you fancy spending time with other dogs and their owners. If you and your clever Siberian are looking for a mental challenge, try rally or tracking; agility is for speed demons and competition obedience is more for the perfectionist.

Rally

Rally obedience, or rally-o, is a combination of agility and traditional obedience. Like agility, rally is timed, and includes 12–20 performance stations. And, once the judge gives the command *"Forward,"* dog and handler complete the course on their own. Like traditional obedience, there are three skill levels, novice, advanced, and excellent. Treats and toys are not allowed in the ring, but handlers can do anything else to encourage their dogs at the novice and advanced levels except physically touch them or make corrections with the leash. Each station's sign instructs the dog-handler team to go fast or slow, halt (dog must sit at heel), make turns or circles, reverse direction, do a *sit-stay-recall*, or follow other basic obedience exercises. Each particular task is performed within 2 to 4 feet (0.6–1.2 m) of the sign. A judge watches for a smooth performance and skill in following station directions and deducts points from the starting 100. If, at the end of the class, two teams have earned the same score, placements are determined by their recorded finishing times. You can go to the AKC's website at *www.akc.org* for more rally information.

Helpful Hints

Working Pack Dog Titles

Both the Siberian Husky Club of America and the Siberian Husky Club of Canada offer both registered and ILP Siberians the Working Pack Dog and Working Pack Dog Excellent titles. See *www.shca.org/shcahp6e.htm* or *www.siberianhusky-clubofcanada.com* for details.

Agility

In its most basic form, agility is a team sport that requires you, the handler, to direct your dog through an obstacle course, off leash, as fast and as precisely as possible using only your voice, body language, and hand signals. The course consists of a set of standard obstacles, laid out by the judge in a 100-by-100-foot (30-by-30-m) area, with numbers indicating the order in which the dog must complete the obstacles. Depending on the type of course, obstacles include tunnels, weave poles, different styles of jumps, an A-frame, a table, a hanging tire, and a teeter-totter. Courses are complex enough that a dog couldn't complete them correctly without handler direction. Jump heights are set according to each competitor's height as

measured at the withers (shoulder). Siberians will generally compete at 20 inches (50 cm)—dogs 22 inches (55 cm) and under at the withers—or 24 inches (60 cm)—dogs over 22 inches (55 cm).

Numerous organizations sanction agility trials and offer titles, including the AKC, the United Kennel Club, the North American Dog Agility Council, and the United States Dog Agility Association. Each of these organizations has slightly different rules and/or course styles, but speed and accuracy are always the bottom line. Competition courses typically contain 12–20 obstacles, with winning times in the 30–50-second range and qualifying times typically 60–70 seconds.

Tracking

Tracking, or trailing, is a mentally stimulating activity for dogs and can help to build their confidence. It is also a rewarding and low-cost activity for you, and something you and your Siberian can do just for fun or in competition. Once you've worked with a scenting dog, you'll come to appreciate the very essence of the canine—their brains are designed to identify smells. And who knows, the experience may lead the two of you to a career in search and rescue or contraband detection. Siberians are not as well known in the tracking field as Bloodhounds, but in 2004 a Siberian became only the 80th dog of ANY breed to earn an AKC Champion Tracker title.

Start by teaching your dog to identify your scent. Trample a small grass area about 2 feet (60 cm) square, the scent pad, with your feet and sprinkle

ACTIVITIES Tracking Titles

Should you and your Siberian get into tracking, he can earn titles offered by both the AKC and the CKC. To learn more, visit *www.akc.org/events/tracking* and *www.ckc.ca.*

U.S. Titles	Track Length	Turns	Track Age	Surface
Tracking Dog (TD)	440–500 yards	3–5	0.5 to 2 hours	Natural
Tracking Dog Excellent (TDX)	800–1000 yards	5–7	3–5 hours	Varied
Variable Surface (VST)	600–800 yards	4–8	3–5 hours	Varied
Champion Tracker (CT)	The dog that has earned the TD, TDX, and VST titles			

Canadian Titles	Track Length	Turns	Track Age	Surface
Tracking Dog (TD)	400–450 meters	2–5	0.5–2 hours	Natural
Tracking Dog Excellent (TDX)	900–1000 meters	5–8	3–5 hours	Varied
Urban Tracking Dog (UTD)	300–400 meters	3–5	1–2 hours	Varied
Urban Tracking Dog Excellent (UTDX)	600–750 meters	5–7	3–5 hours	Varied
Tracking Champion (TCh)	A dog that has earned the TD, TDX, UTD, and UTDX			

a few tiny treats in the scent pad. With your Siberian on leash, encourage him to nose around on the scent pad and find the treats. Next, lay a short, straight track. First, trample a scent pad and put a single treat in it. Then, taking overlapping baby steps, walk out 6 feet (1.8 m) and make another smaller scent pad and put a treat in it. Go get your dog and encourage him to find the first treat and to follow the short track to the second treat. Praise lavishly when he finds it.

Increase distance and complexity over time by lengthening the distance between treats and introducing turns into the tracks. Most dogs will over-shoot a turn at first, so make it easy for your Siberian by putting a second treat in the track about 6 feet (1.8 m) beyond the turn to give him something to follow. Once your Siberian gets the hang of it and you're laying longer and more complex tracks, phase out the number of treats and scent pads along the track and put one big, extra special treat at the very end. Make a big, big deal of praising your dog when he gets to the end of the track.

Obedience

Today's competition obedience can be all about precision, almost canine dressage, demanding tremendous mental effort from both human and dog—if that's what you want. If your goal is simply to build a bond between you and your Siberian and to enjoy the process, you can do that too. At the novice level, the dog demonstrates walking on a leash at his owner's side, standing to be touched by a stranger, sitting and lying down with distractions, and coming when called. Advanced classes are designed to prove your ability to train your Siberian to retrieve, jump, obey hand signals, and discriminate scent. Every dog walks into the ring with a perfect score of 200. Judges then deduct points when a dog walks out of heel position, sits too slowly or not at all, or breaks position on the *stand*, *sit*, or *down* exercises. Judges also deduct points for handler errors, such as tugging on the leash or giving more than one command for a single exercise. A dog earns a "leg" by receiving a qualifying score of more than 50 percent of the available points for each exercise and at least 170 total points. Three legs under

three different judges earn the Beginner Novice (BN), Companion Dog (CD), Companion Dog Excellent (CDX), and Utility Dog (UD) titles. The Utility Dog Excellent (UDX) and Obedience Trial Champion (OTCh) titles can be earned by top-scoring teams who love to compete. The Canadian Kennel Club offers equivalent titles.

Obedience trials are hosted by obedience training clubs or kennel clubs and are often held in conjunction with conformation shows. You can attend an obedience trial as a spectator to become familiar with ring procedure and ask questions of experienced exhibitors, but you can't bring your Siberian with you. Not to worry, though, because training clubs also regularly schedule informal events, called matches, where you and your Siberian can practice in a simulated trial environment.

Conformation

Chances are, if you're an Animal Planet channel watcher, you've seen televised dog shows such as Westminster or the AKC/Eukanuba Championship, and maybe even watched the Siberians being judged. Did you wonder if your Siberian could have won that big purple-and-gold rosette? To be eligible to compete at a conformation show, a dog must: be individually registered with the American Kennel Club (or its equivalent), be six months of age or older on the day of the show, and meet any eligibility requirements in the written standard for his breed. Some breed standards, including the Siberian Husky's, have a height restriction. To compete, Siberian males cannot be over 23.5 inches (58.75 cm) tall at the withers; females not over 22 inches (55 cm) tall. Additionally, spayed or neutered dogs are not eligible to compete in conformation classes at a dog show, because the purpose of a dog show is to evaluate breeding stock.

At a dog show such as Westminster, a judge evaluates the dogs, then gives awards according to how closely each dog compares to the judge's mental image of the "perfect" dog described in the breed's official standard (page 167), which includes specifications for structure, temperament, and movement. Most dogs are competing for points toward their championships. In the United States, it takes fifteen points, including two majors (wins of three, four, or five points) awarded by at least three different judges, to become a "Champion of Record." The number of championship points awarded depends on the number of males (dogs) and females (bitches) of the breed actually in competition—the larger the entry, the greater the number of points, up to a maximum of five. Males and females compete separately within their respective breeds, in seven regular classes.

Showing your Siberian to his championship will not be cheap, so if you want to seriously consider doing so, you need to have an experienced Siberian owner evaluate your dog for you. If, in the opinion of your Siberian's breeder, or the experienced Siberian owner, your dog has the conformation to be competitive, you'll need to learn how to present your dog in a conformation ring. Local kennel clubs and dog training clubs hold regular conformation training classes.

Siberians as Therapists

Siberians just know. They know that their gentle touch can bring comfort to a person who's suffered loss. They seem to sense vulnerability and behave appropriately. Siberians are accepting, nonjudgmental, and forgiving of mistakes, and they offer unconditional love to all they meet. They enjoy human contact and are content to be petted and handled, sometimes clumsily, because they seem to instinctively know they're there to allow strangers to make physical contact with them and to enjoy that contact.

The most important characteristic of a therapy dog is his temperament. A therapy dog must get along remarkably well with children, men, women, and other animals. The dog must also be friendly, confident, patient, calm, gentle, and receptive to training. Socialization (being confident and comfortable in most situations and places) is essential for all dogs, but it is especially important for a dog to be considered for a therapy program. Your Siberian will need to be accustomed to children, who enjoy hugging, and adults, who usually want to pet him. Your Siberian may be asked to be the nonjudgmental ears to a child who

Helpful Hints

Therapy Dog Certification

There are numerous therapy dog organizations, but virtually all of them use the certification requirements of Therapy Dogs International (*www.tdi.org*) or The Delta Society (*www.deltasociety.org*). Note that therapy dogs are not considered by U.S. law to have the same status as service dogs.

has difficulty reading, or he might need to carefully climb onto a hospital bed and sit or lie there quietly.

If you're interested in becoming a therapy team with your Siberian, you'll both need to complete thorough training. General obedience training is a very necessary beginning, but therapy dogs must also be comfortable with elevators, escalators, and the high-pitched whine of a respirator. They must be able to handle sudden loud or strange noises, walk on unfamiliar surfaces comfortably, and be at ease around people with canes, wheelchairs, or unusual styles of walking or moving. Therapy dogs pay no attention to strange smells, food, toys, or medications while they work. And finally, because the safety and welfare of your Siberian Husky is paramount, you must learn how to handle unexpected situations and protect your dog from harm.

The Great White Outdoors

Siberians were made for winter. As far as they are concerned, there is nothing better than tunneling through a fresh snowdrift or flying down a snow-covered trail just to see what's around the next curve. If you own a Siberian AND live in an area that has regular snowfall and adequate snow cover for most of the winter, you are in the enviable position of being able to participate in your Siberian's natural calling: winter travel. For him, the fun is in the traveling; the adventure is over upon arrival. Siberians love to run, and they are built to run on snow. Gliding almost silently through a frozen forest, hearing only soft panting and the zing of runners on snow, is exhilarating. Your biggest challenges will be deciding which of the winter sports you and your Siberian want to participate in, and training your dog to lead.

Skijoring/Pulka/Canicross

Skijoring and pulka, very popular winter sports in Scandinavia and Alaska for years, are spreading to all corners of the world as dog enthusiasts realize they are activities one can participate in with one dog and minimal equipment. First, of course, you need to be a competent cross-country skier. The cross-country skier provides power with skis and poles, and the dog adds additional power by running and pulling. If your skiing technique needs honing, practice by being towed behind a sled dog team or snowmobile. The skier wears a skijoring belt, the dog wears a sled dog harness, and the two are connected by a length of rope. Like all sled dog sports, there are no reins or other signaling devices to keep the dog on the trail in front of you on a taut line. Training your dog to skijor is best done before you put on your skis, to avoid being catapulted into trees, snowbanks, or half-frozen creeks.

Equipment is minimal, consisting of a standard nylon web racing-style harness and a towline for the dog, and a skijor belt and cross-country skis for you. Don't use the harnesses carried by pet supply stores—they are not designed for pulling. One end of the towline attaches to your dog's harness and the other end to either a tow bar à la water skiing or, more commonly and safely, to your skijor belt. A towline-to-belt arrangement improves your balance by lowering your center of gravity and frees your hands to use poles. The towline can be fitted with a shock cord or bungee to lessen jerks as skier and dog go over bumps or around turns.

All sled dog sports will require you to teach your Siberian to pull, yet you have just spent months teaching your dog NOT to pull on leash. No worries. Your Siberian has the running gene, and the towline is attached to the back of his harness, not his collar, so teaching him to pull while in harness will not be a problem. Enlist two helpers, one to start your dog and one to run down the trail ahead of him. Choose a trail that is safe and flat, has no sharp turns, is well defined, and is free of vehicular traffic. When you arrive at the trail-head, put on your skijor belt and connect the towline, then harness your dog and attach the towline to his harness. Choke up on the line so you are closer to your dog for control. DO NOT wrap the towline around your hands. Have your helper lead your dog, by the collar or harness, to the trail and hold your dog forward, keeping the towline taut. Have the "chasee" jog up the trail while calling your dog by name until he starts bouncing and yowling. You want him to want to chase! When the chasee is about 40 yards (36.6 m) up the trail, say, "Let's go!" or "All right!" and, keeping the line taut, begin moving forward behind your dog. If he responds by lunging forward, immediately say, "Good dog!" and, all the while keeping the towline taut, let him gain speed by increasing your speed behind him. Without letting the line go slack, slowly play out the choked-up line to its full length.

Helpful Hints

Skijoring/Pulka/Canicross Resourses

Ski Spot Run by Matt Haakenstad and John Thompson

Skijor with Your Dog by Carol Kaynor, Mari Hoe-Raitto

Dog Driver by Miki and Julie Collins

www.alaskaskijoring.org
Alaska Skijor and Pulk Association

www.psdsa.org
Pacific Sled Dog and Skijor Association

www.sleddogcentral.com
Sled Dog Central—source of sled dog sports information

Then your Siberian will need to learn the classic sledding commands to start running ("Hike," "Let's go," "All right"), to turn right and left ("Gee" and "Haw"), to stop on command (good luck with that) and to pass distractions ("On by" or "Leave it"). You'll also need to teach your dog to pass, and to be passed by, other teams of dogs, horses, or skiers without interfering with them. You do not want your dog to stop to chat with another team passing you at high speed—even one dog can pull a skier at 12 miles per hour (7 kph) or better, and three dogs can easily run 20 miles per hour (12 kph) for short distances. A well-trained sled dog will pass a distraction without even turning his head.

Finding a local skijoring group will make mastering this sport much easier for both you and your Siberian, and help you avoid novice training mistakes. More important, you will have a chance to observe, and possibly skijor with a trained dog. And the camaraderie of skijoring with other teams will be especially enjoyable for your Siberian, who is, after all, a team dog at heart. Should you decide to compete, exposure to other skijoring teams in a recreational setting will prepare both of you for the race environment.

Pulka is essentially skijoring with the addition of a driverless sled called a pulk, and a special harness system for your dog. The dog pulls the sled while the skier skis behind the pulk, or in between the dog and pulk, to steer and brake if necessary. All three (dog, pulk, and skier) are attached by lines. Although you can certainly use a child's plastic toboggan as a pulk, special care is absolutely necessary to prevent the sled from hitting your dog.

Skijoring is practiced recreationally, and competitively, both for long-distance travel and for short (sprint) distances. Skijor competitions associated with sprint races offer classes for one-, two-, and three-dog teams with distances of three to ten miles (4.8–16 km). Most sled dog clubs have a skijoring contingent, and there are a few clubs devoted to skijoring only. Pulka racing is still primarily a European activity, but backwoods and distance skijorers in North America have taken to using pulks to haul camping and survival gear.

The word *canicross* is a combination of *canine* and *cross-country*, as in cross-country running. Canicross is skijoring on dry land, land without snow. As in skijoring, your dog's harness is attached to your belt by a length of rope, and his pull adds distance to your running stride as well as a little help on the uphills. Canicross is best known in the United Kingdom and European countries, but is gaining popularity with dog drivers in North America as a way to keep both dogs and drivers fit and trained during months when there is no snow. Because it can be part of a sensible fitness program for dogs and their people, top runners and average Joes who just want an inexpensive and fun way to spend time outside with their dogs are also avid canicross fans. Canicross events, especially for children, are routinely offered at fall rig (wheeled cart) races across Europe. Events are also being held in the United Kingdom and Canada, and are beginning to show up more often across the United States.

Breed Truths

Distinctive Collars

Using different collars for different activities will help alleviate confusion for your dog. Your Siberian will quickly realize that his racing collar means he's going skijoring and should pull, his regular collar means he walks next to you on leash, and the fancy collar means he needs to be on his best therapy visit behavior.

Sledding

The ultimate Siberian winter sport has to be sledding, because, as mentioned earlier, your Siberian is a team dog at heart. Although a single dog can pull a lightweight sled and equally lightweight musher, he can't do it very far or very fast. A three-dog team will allow driver and dogs to cover miles of groomed trail without working too hard; a five- or six-dog team can haul a loaded sled at a fast trot for hours. Sledding can be recreational, competitive, or work related—whatever the dog driver desires, from a single dog and child running 100-yard (90-m) dashes, to a 6-dog team on a winter camping trip, to a 10-dog wilderness patrol team, to a 16-dog Iditarod team running more than 1,100 miles (1,760 km) in 10 days, to a 20-dog sprint team racing 35 miles (56 km) per day for three days.

Driving a team of dogs, even if it is a small team, requires more advanced training skills. You'll be standing on two narrow pieces of wood (the runners of the sled), holding on to a handlebar (the driving bow). The lead dog(s) on

ACTIVITIES Sled Dog Titles

In an effort to preserve the working capabilities of the breed, both the Siberian Husky Club of America and the Siberian Husky Club of Canada award racing titles to registered Siberian Huskies. In August 2010, the AKC recognized the SHCA's Sled Dog Degree Program. See *www.shca.org* or *www.siberianhuskyclubofcanada.com* for detailed rules and eligibility.

American Titles

Sled Dog (S.D.): Accumulate at least 100 miles (160 km) in at least five races with qualifying times within 1.33 times the average finishing time of the top three Purebred teams in the same class.

Sled Dog Excellent (S.D.X.): An additional 150 miles (240 km) in at least five races with qualifying times within 1.29 times the average finishing time of the top three teams in the same class.

Sled Dog Outstanding (S.D.O.): An additional 200 miles (320 km) in at least five races with qualifying times within 1.25 times the average finishing time of the top three teams in the same class.

Canadian Titles

Sled Dog (S.D.): Sledding at least 50 miles (80 km) in three successful races.

Sled Dog Excellent (S.D.X.): Sledding an additional 100 miles (160 km) in three successful races.

Sled Dog Unlimited (SDU): Sledding an additional 300 miles (480 km) in three successful races.

a three-dog team will be 20 feet (6 m) in front of you. Each additional pair of dogs adds 8 feet (2.4 m) to the length of your team. A 16-dog team, the size used by most Iditarod mushers, is more than 70 feet (21 m) long from lead dogs to the back of the sled. You'll need a trained lead dog—remember, there are no reins!—because it is essential that you have adequate control of your dogs, for their safety and your own. There are numerous books on the sport, but by far the best way to learn how to drive a sled, train multiple dogs to work as a team, and care for them properly is to find a mentor. Most northern tier and coastal states in the United States, and all provinces in Canada, have sled dog clubs where you can meet experienced mushers who are happy to share their passion for sledding with you.

Just as canicross is essentially skijoring on dry land, rig racing is essentially sledding on dry land, using a lightweight three- or four-wheeled cart instead of a sled. Most everything, including training principles and conditioning requirements, is the same for both dry-land and snow sledding. The dogs are attached to a rig the same way they are attached to a sled, with the driver either sitting or standing, depending on the rig's construction. The dry-land racing season is often longer than a snow racing season, trails are generally shorter, and the teams are smaller. Race rules are also generally the same, except for temperature and humidity restrictions. Race-giving organizations generally cancel when temperatures climb above 50°F/10°C, depending on the humidity.

In this day and age, your ability to keep even a small sled dog team may be restricted by several factors, including financial considerations and municipal ordinances limiting the number of animals housed at a residence. Remember that your Siberians are not sports equipment that can be put away at the end of the season—they are dogs who need appropriate year-round care. Before adding to your Siberian pack, be sure your local laws allow the number of dogs you're planning for, and that you have, and will have, the finances to properly care for all your dogs 365 days a year for their entire lives, even when their racing careers are over.

All sled dog sports require year-round conditioning for dog and driver. While training during warmer months, you must be watchful for signs of heat stress, especially when temperatures are above 40°F (4.5°C). Keep sessions short and always have fresh water on hand. An old musher's adage, "No Feet, No Dog," bears repeating. A sled dog is only as good as his feet, so keep an eye on your dogs' feet to head off problems. What you feed, how often you feed, and how much depends greatly on what sort of sledding your dogs are engaged in. Dogs that travel day after day will need a different diet from those who run 5 miles (8 km) on a weekend. Talk to experienced mushers and read everything you can find on the subject of sled dog nutrition. Remember that control of your team is 100 percent your responsibility, not your dogs'. If you aren't sure you can handle two dogs yet, don't hook up three. Be sure dogs are welcome on the trails you use, and clean up after your dog(s) before you leave. And most important, have fun with your Siberian(s).

Helpful Hints

Sledding Resourses

The details of conditioning, training, and caring for sled dogs are beyond the scope of this book. The following books and websites offer some information and links to more.

Mush! A Beginner's Manual, edited by B. Levorsen for Sierra Nevada Dog Drivers, Inc.

Dog Driver by Miki and Julie Collins

The World of Sled Dogs by Lorna Coppinger

Racing Alaskan Sled Dogs, compiled by Bill Vaudrin

www.isdra.org International Sled Dog Racing Association

www.isdvma.org International Sled Dog Veterinary Medical Association

www.sleddogsport.net International Federation of Sleddog Sports

www.mushwithpride.org PRIDE (Providing Responsible Information on a Dog's Environment)

www.sleddogcentral.com Sled Dog Central—central website for equipment, books, and clubs

Leash Training

1 Put a collar on your dog and attach a short, soft leash that you can gather up in your hand. Start with your dog at your left knee. Use your left hand and the leash to keep the dog in position, allowing him to neither surge ahead nor lag behind as you walk slowly forward. If you are training a small puppy, you may need to bend over.

2 Lure your dog forward with a tiny piece of treat and give it to him. Continue luring and giving him small treats every few steps. Adjust your stride and speed to the dog's stride length while keeping him at your left knee with the leash.

3 If he stops or fights against the leash, you stop, but say and do nothing. When he relaxes, continue to walk and lure him with the treat and verbal praise. As long as the leash has some slack, say *"Good boy,"* and keep walking.

4 As he gets better at walking beside you, lengthen the leash and phase out the treats by simply substituting verbal praise. Be consistent, even as you add distractions—when he takes the slack out of the leash by charging ahead after a squirrel or lagging behind to sniff a bush, stop walking instantly. Until he returns to your side, stand still.

141

The Sit Command

1 Start with the dog in front of you, and the short, soft leash and a small treat in your right hand. If he's a small puppy, you may want to kneel on one knee.

2 Hold the leash straight up with your right hand, **gently** push down on the dog's rump with your left hand, and say *"Sit"* in a clear, matter-of-fact tone. As soon as your Siberian's rear is on the floor, say "Good" and give him the treat, but don't let him stand up immediately.

3 Once he starts to bend his knees in response to your "*Sit*" command, you can gradually omit **gently** pushing his rump down. When he puts his rump on the floor in response to "*Sit,*" you can gradually omit holding the leash straight up. Reward every positive response with praise and a treat.

4 Continue to practice on leash until he sits every time you tell him to. Only then will you practice the *sit* command off leash in a secure location.

The Stay Command

1 Attach the short leash to your dog's collar, put him in a *sit*, and stand directly in front of him. After one or two seconds, if your dog is still in the *sit*, give him a treat and calm praise. You are rewarding the behavior you want, which is a *stay*, even if it is for only one or two seconds.

2 Begin the process again from the start, this time for three to five seconds. If your dog breaks out of the *stay* at any time, don't give the treat or praise, but simply start the process again for two to three seconds.

3 Now add the hand signal and verbal command *"Stay"* to Step 1. Put your dog in a *sit* and stand directly in front of him. Say *"Stay"* and at the same time hold your hand out in front of you, with your palm facing your dog's nose. Wait a second or two, then praise and reward. Repeat this step over and over, gradually increasing the time between your *stay* command and your praise and treat.

4 Say *"Stay"* and use your hand signal, then take a step backward without tugging on the leash. Pause for a second, then step back to your dog and praise him. Repeat and gradually increase the distance you step back, using longer leashes. Remember to return to your dog before you reward him. Introduce distractions and new locations after your dog can *sit-stay* reliably for a minute or more.

Chapter Eight

Grooming a Siberian Husky

Coat Care

Being a true northern dog, the Siberian has a double coat consisting of a thick, soft undercoat and an outer coat of longer, coarse guard hairs. The guard hairs are naturally oily and, in winter, can produce a fleeting, faint charcoal smell in the fur when your dog comes inside from a romp in the cold. More important, the naturally occurring oils in the outer coat provide a measure of water resistance, a survival trait in arctic climates where staying dry is a matter of life or death. Moisture and dirt tend to collect on the guard hairs, whereas the undercoat stays clean and dry. A good shake is usually all it takes to remove snow, dust, or dirt from the outer coat. As a result, the Siberian is a naturally clean dog and should never develop a "doggie" odor. If your Siberian lives in your home, he will need, at most, two baths a year.

Bath time for this breed is usually late spring, coinciding with the shedding of the undercoat. Most breeds of dogs shed, but the Siberian produces a veritable hair explosion—hence the term *blowing coat*. The quantity of hair on a Siberian is so abundant that some owners collect and spin it into enough yarn to make a hat and matching scarf. If dog hair in your house is an issue, this should be a factor when deciding whether to acquire a Siberian Husky.

Shedding occurs over the course of six to eight weeks, starting with visible tufting on the legs, and moves up the body to the topline. The hair of the tail and britches (longer hair on the rear of the thigh) is usually the last to become loose. Loose hair on the haunches, neck, and tail will form mats without regular combing. You can speed up the shedding process with a warm soak or two, and vigorous daily brushing.

As soon as you see that first tuft of loose hair, comb your dog from head to tail. The best tool for this job is a "greyhound" comb—a stainless-steel comb with 1 1/8-inch (28-mm) teeth, widely spaced on one half and closely spaced on the other. Several brands are available at most good pet stores, especially those carrying dog-showing supplies. Use the widely spaced tooth side of your comb first, to untangle and loosen dead hair. Switch to the closely spaced tooth side and comb your Siberian until you can run the comb through his coat quickly, in any direction, without resistance. If your

SHOPPING LIST

Grooming Supplies

The Siberian is a wash-and-wear dog, no endless grooming required. You'll need the following to keep your dog groomed to the nines:

Must have
- ✔ Greyhound comb
- ✔ Pin brush
- ✔ Nail clippers and styptic powder
- ✔ Scissors (small, sharp)
- ✔ Shampoo formulated for dogs
- ✔ Toothbrush and toothpaste formulated for dogs

Nice to have
- ✔ Coat rake
- ✔ Tangle remover (liquid)
- ✔ Self-rinsing shampoo
- ✔ Ambient-air, high-velocity blow dryer
- ✔ Grooming table and arm

dog seems to blow his entire undercoat all at once, you might consider investing in an undercoat rake to get at the denser parts of the coat. The rake has very widely spaced teeth positioned at a right angle to its handle, and is specifically designed to pull dense, loose undercoat through guard hair. With a gentle but firm touch, rake about a 6-inch (15-cm) swath at a time.

If you find a mat, first separate it lengthwise into two mats with your fingers. Keep pulling the mats apart into smaller mats until you can gently

untangle them with a comb. Tangle remover, a liquid available at pet stores, may be helpful if your Siberian's coat mats easily. Putting your dog up on a grooming table, picnic table, or other stable, elevated platform will make grooming an easier daily process for your back and indicate to the dog that this isn't playtime.

As shedding progresses, a timely bath will clean the skin, hasten the removal of loose hair, and accelerate the loosening of dead, but still attached, hair. Shampoos formulated for humans are not suitable for use on Siberians. A dog's skin has an alkaline ph, whereas human skin has an acidic ph. Human products will irritate your dog's skin and excessively dry out his coat. Use a good shampoo formulated for dogs, or diluted dish soap: three parts water to one part liquid soap. Don't bathe your Siberian with flea shampoo unless he has fleas!

In warm weather, you can bathe your Siberian outside, using a kiddie pool and a garden hose. If the planned bath includes a warm soak to hasten shedding, or the weather is cool, you'll want to bathe your dog in a bathtub or enclosed shower stall using a handheld sprayer attached to the faucet or showerhead. In either case, save the face and ears for last.

Water

Siberians are not natural water dogs. Even in the hottest weather, your Siberian may refuse to wade in the baby pool you thoughtfully bought, and some will actively resist being forced to swim or have a bath. Positive experiences with water in puppyhood will make bathing your adult Siberian easier—for you and your dog.

Begin just behind the ears, working back and down, to wet your dog to the skin. He will want to follow the sprayer with his nose, so lift his muzzle

Helpful Hints

Self-Rinsing Shampoo

Keep a small bottle of self-rinsing shampoo handy should you need something stronger than water to clean your Siberian's face. This type of shampoo is tearless and does not need to be rinsed out, so you needn't worry about getting water in your Siberian's ears after you've washed out the grass stains.

slightly above parallel to keep water out of his ears while you are drenching his neck. Work the lather through the coat to the skin, paying particular attention to the longer hair of his ruff (coat around his neck), haunches (the hip and thigh), and tail. Use a nail brush on his legs and feet if they are very dirty. Rinse thoroughly, working down and back from the neck, then rinse some more. Every trace of shampoo must be removed to prevent soap residue from burning your Siberian's skin. A wet cloth, rinsed often, is all you will normally need to clean his face and external ears.

The advantage of bathing your Siberian outside is that when he shakes, the water that flies out of his coat is outside as well. If he's been bathed in the bathtub, keep one hand on his head while you quickly pull the shower curtain closed, then let him shake once or twice before toweling. Your Siberian will race around, roll, and shake vigorously after a bath, so towel-dry him as much as possible before turning him loose in the house, and don't turn him loose in the yard if it's wet or muddy. Be aware that it can take between

10 and 12 hours for a Siberian in full coat to air-dry, even longer in humid climates. So, if you don't want a damp dog in the house for that long, an ambient-air, high-velocity dog dryer is your friend. In addition to blowing water out of your Siberian's coat, these high-velocity dryers are powerful enough to blow dead hair and loose dander right off the dog. During the height of shedding season, 15 minutes every other day, a pin brush, and the dryer will do wonders to keep your Siberian's hair outside—where songbirds can use it as nesting material. Dryers also make it easier for you to inspect your Siberian's skin for ticks and sores.

A final word about your Siberian's coat: Although you might think shaving your Siberian in summer will make him more comfortable, you would be wrong. The Siberian's coat insulates him from both excessive heat and cold, and it protects his skin from the sun and insects. As long as your Siberian has adequate ventilation, available shade, and fresh water, he will be just fine in even the warmest climate. Removing the coat will make it difficult for your dog to regulate his body temperature, and will leave his skin exposed to sunburn and every insect that flies by. Except for medical reasons, the Siberian's coat is not to be cut or shaved—ever.

Ear Care

Siberians are not usually prone to ear infections or ear mites, and because the inside of the ear is well furred, cuts and scrapes are rare. Still, bath time is another perfect opportunity to clean and inspect the crannies of the exter-

CAUTION

Lyme Disease

The best way to prevent Lyme disease is to keep ticks off your dog, but if you can't, make sure you check for ticks often and remove them within 48 hours. There are serious questions about the efficacy and side effects of currently available Lyme disease vaccines, including kidney failure and symptoms similar to the disease itself. Talk with your veterinarian before agreeing to vaccinate.

nal ear for ticks and burrs. Wipe only the parts of his ears you can see using a wet cloth, and never stick a cotton swab down his ear canal. If you see excessive wax, clean it out with ear cleaner from your veterinarian, and should excessive wax become a chronic problem, seek veterinary help. If you see your dog shaking his head repeatedly, pawing at his ear, tilting his head at an odd angle, or holding an ear strangely, check for ticks, an injury, or an infection. Redness and pain in the ear, a foul odor, or a buildup of dark debris in the ear signal infections best taken care of by a veterinarian. If your Siberian spends a lot of time outdoors, particularly in farm or horse country, and you see specks of dried blood on the tips of his ears, think fly bites. Horseflies, blackflies, and deerflies are the most common culprits. The best treatment for this problem is prevention, which consists of applying a topical insect repellant to your Siberian's ear tips. Pyrethrin or permethrin ointments, and homemade pyrethrin and petroleum jelly mixes are very effective in repelling flies.

Skin Problems and Allergies

The most prevalent skin problem in the breed is "hot spots," also known as acute moist dermatitis or moist eczema. Hot spots tend to occur most often in the summer months, seem to appear spontaneously anywhere on your Siberian's body, and can spread rapidly. Anything—an insect bite, a scratch, a thorn prick—that irritates or breaks the skin can cause a hot spot. The body's natural response is to itch or become inflamed. The itching causes the dog to scratch, chew, and lick the area, further damaging the skin and creating the moist environment needed for bacterial infection to set in. Fortunately, most of the bacteria cultured from hot spots respond to oral and topical antibiotics. Look for incessant scratching, chewing, or licking at one area or a bare spot with red, moist skin and a film of pus, surrounded by hair wet from saliva. Treatment includes cleaning the area with an antiseptic, stopping the itch, and letting the sore dry out. Check with your veterinarian for recommendations of over-the-counter anti-itch products that can be helpful in breaking the itch-scratch cycle. For the hot spot to heal, your Siberian must stop licking it, so use an Elizabethan collar (a rigid plastic cone attached to his usual collar—shown in the photo on page 67) to prevent access. Seek veterinary assistance if necessary to keep the infection from getting out of hand.

Seasonal allergies and food allergies are not common problems found in the Siberian. Flea allergy dermatitis, the most common allergy among dogs in general, is also rarely seen in the breed, but flea bites can cause hot spots, and severe flea infestations can trigger flea bite hypersensitivity in predisposed dogs. Keep fleas and ticks off your Siberian.

External Parasites

A healthy Siberian is a flea-and-tick-free Siberian, and it is much less expensive to prevent these pests from infesting your dog than it is to treat the hot spot or tapeworm he can get from fleas, or the host of diseases he can get from ticks.

It can be very difficult to see fleas in a Siberian Husky's dense undercoat, so you will need to watch for scratching and biting and look carefully for flea dirt on his head, at the base of his tail, and at the spot he is scratching. Ticks can often be felt, so if you feel an unusual bump, or your nail catches on "something" as you're scratching your dog behind the ears or rubbing his belly, separate the hair and take a look. Although flea and tick sprays, dips, flea collars, and natural remedies are generally ineffective or unsafe for Siberians, a variety of safe and effective products on the market today kill and/or repel fleas, ticks, or both. Look for products with residual effects lasting one to three months, and be especially careful to read and follow label directions. Products designed for use on adult dogs should not be used on puppies; products designed for other species should not be used on dogs. Topical products typically contain permethrin, imidaloprid, fipronil, or selamectin. Lufenuron, an oral medication, interrupts the flea's reproductive cycle once it bites, but does not kill the flea. Nitenpyram, another oral medication, kills the fleas on your dog within half an hour but does not prevent new infestations. Spinosad is a monthly oral medication that kills fleas quickly and has residual effects that help prevent reinfestation. Most important, remember that not all products are right for all dogs under all circumstances. Experts caution against the indiscriminant use of any parasite-control product, so select products that target only the parasites found in your area and use them only when necessary. Talk to your veterinarian, use these chemicals only as directed, and rotate products to reduce the chance that fleas will develop a resistance to any one chemical. And if you live, or exercise your Siberian, in tick-infested areas, check him over regularly. If you find a tick on your Siberian, remove it immediately by grasping the pest as close to the dog's skin as possible and pulling it straight out. Spraying the tick with insecticide, burning it with a match, or applying oil to smother it is not recommended.

Nail and Foot Care

The only hair the Siberian doesn't shed can be found on the bottoms of his feet, between the pads. This hair grows continuously and is a magnet for mud, ice-and-snow-melt chemicals, thorns, burrs, and splinters. Using small, sharp scissors, keep this hair trimmed flush with the pads of the feet. Keeping the hair between his pads short will also allow you to see cuts, thorns, or sores more easily should your Siberian suddenly start to lick or chew on a foot or develop a limp. If your Siberian walks on ice-and-snow-melt chemicals in the winter, wash his feet in soapy water before he has a chance to lick them. Many of these products are caustic and/or poisonous.

Active Siberians, who have regular access to rough pavement, may need their nails trimmed only three or four times a year. Still, you should check your Siberian's feet regularly and trim his nails when needed. If your

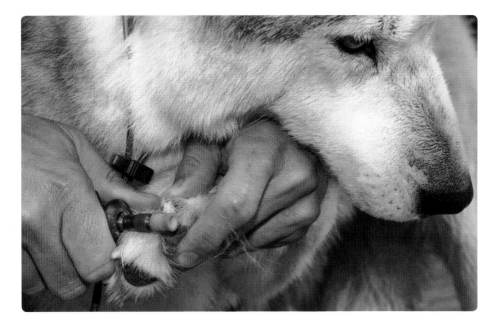

Siberian has dewclaws, you will need to trim the nails on these rudimentary toes more often. As a rule, Siberians do not like their feet or legs touched, so trimming your adult Siberian's nails might be easier if you spend time touching his feet and pretending to cut his nails when he is a puppy. Toweling his feet when he comes in out of the rain or snow presents another opportunity to get him used to having his feet touched, and may help set the stage for peaceful nail trimming. There are two types of mechanical nail clippers sturdy enough to cut Siberian toenails: the guillotine type and the safety type. An electric nail grinder is also an option. Grinders are available from veterinary/show supply houses. Make sure, if you use nail clippers, that they are sharp. Dull clippers crush and splinter the nail instead of cutting cleanly, and that hurts your dog.

The sensitive quick of the toenail extends a bit beyond the reddish area inside the nail that indicates where the blood supply ends. To avoid cutting into the quick, cut the nail where it starts to look hollow. Some Siberians have one or more opaque black toenails, so when in doubt, cut less now and shave a bit more off in two weeks or so. Have a container of styptic powder on hand in case you do accidentally cut into the quick. Pack and hold a pinch of powder into the cut area of the nail for a moment or two to stop the bleeding. Styptic powder does not sting your dog. An electric nail grinder uses an emery paper loop to quickly grind the nail to a smooth finish, and Siberians easily adapt to the noise and slight vibration. Grinders do create dust, so if this is an issue, you'll want to wear eye protection and a dust mask. Ideally, your Siberian's nails should not click on the floor when he walks. If you have never trimmed a dog's nails before, a professional groomer or your veterinarian can show you how to do it safely and properly.

Dental Care

Some Siberians have pearly whites that stay that way their entire lives with little or no brushing, whereas others have significant tartar buildup on their teeth within months of a professional cleaning. Keeping your dog's teeth clean is essential for good health, especially as he ages. Tartar buildup leads to bad breath and periodontal disease, which can cause tooth loss and systemic infection.

Oral Disease

According to the American Veterinary Dental Society, 80 percent of dogs show signs of oral disease by age three, and it is the most common health problem treated in small-animal health clinics today. Regular cleaning will keep your Siberian in the 20 percent with no periodontal disease!

Chew toys and crunchy foods may help remove some plaque, the precursor to tartar, but regular brushing is necessary to prevent tartar from forming. You can have your veterinarian clean your dog's teeth under anesthesia, or you can easily do it yourself, but don't use human toothpaste or household baking soda. The ingredients in these products will make your dog sick.

Tooth scalers and tooth-brushing kits designed especially for dogs are available at pet stores and from your veterinarian. Finger toothbrushes, which fit over your index finger, may be easier for you to use and more acceptable to your dog than a hard plastic toothbrush with a handle. Dog toothpaste comes in beef, chicken, and other tasty flavors, and if you start brushing your Siberian's teeth in puppyhood, he may even look forward to

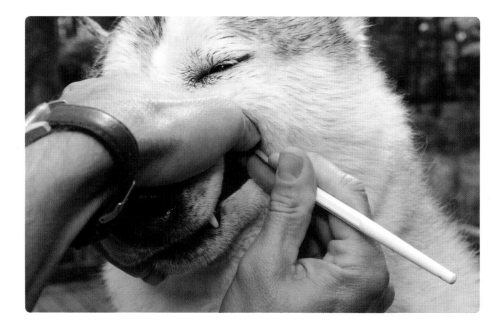

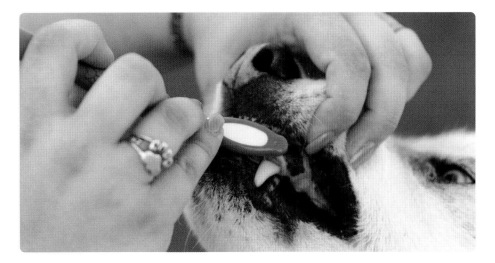

it. Start by offering your puppy a taste of the toothpaste. Next time, let him taste the toothpaste, then run your finger along the gums of the upper teeth. The next time, repeat the whole process and add the toothbrush. Position the bristles along the gum line of the upper back teeth and angle slightly up, so the bristles can get under the gum line. Work from back to front, making small circles along the gum lines. It should take less than 30 seconds to brush your Siberian's teeth. Brushing at least twice a week should keep your Siberian's teeth clean and bright, but if brushing isn't enough, you may need to scale his teeth occasionally. Ask your veterinarian or a professional groomer for specific instructions on using tooth scalers. Giving your Siberian a dog biscuit a day will not keep his teeth clean, but it will make the dog happy!

You will also want to check your Siberian's mouth regularly for chipped or broken teeth, sores or growths, or bleeding. Abnormalities will need to be seen by your veterinarian. If your dog looks as if he wants to eat but won't, or paws at his mouth, check for tooth infection or a foreign object in his mouth.

Breed Truths

Toys

Siberian teeth can slice through the average supermarket dog toy in a matter of seconds, posing choking and obstruction hazards. Plush toys last only as long as it takes him to pull all the stuffing out. Squeaky toys should be offered only under close supervision—you must grab the squeaker before he swallows it. Consider all balls tennis sized and smaller a choking hazard. Rawhide chews are devoured quickly, and linked to intestinal blockage. Provide your Siberian with chew toys designed for powerful chewers—durable toys he can't bite into pieces but that satisfy his need to chew and help clean his teeth. Chews made of nylon, polyurethane, or very strong rubber are the most popular Siberian-tested, owner-approved choices.

Chapter Nine

The Senior Siberian

T ime flies when you're having fun, and suddenly your Siberian is, well, elderly. Where did those 13, 14, or 15 years go? Barring a catastrophic illness or injury, Siberians are a long-lived breed, and especially when properly fed and kept active, they tend to stay healthy well into their teens. Still, every senior Siberian will require some extra time and attention to stay happy in his golden years.

Safe and Healthy Aging

Siberians are not known for slowing down much as they age, but that doesn't mean you'll want to take your 14-year-old on a ten-mile (16 km) bike ride in the middle of summer. He does need exercise, because inactivity will cause him to lose muscle mass and tone, which will make it more difficult for him to move, so he'll move less, and a vicious cycle will start. Your Siberian needs exercise to maintain a healthy weight, stay flexible, and keep the muscles around his joints strong. But, to avoid overdoing it when he does start to slow down, try low-impact exercises such as moderate walking several times a day. If your Siberian is a retriever, a gentle game of fetch with your old guy could be fun, but remember to include more rest periods during exercise. And if your senior is developing arthritis, using a ramp to get into and out of the car will take the stress off his joints.

Your Siberian also needs as much mental stimulation in later life as he did when he was younger. An activity such as tracking, which features both low-impact exercise and mental stimulation, is something to consider for older dogs. Your Siberian may become less insistent about being with you as he ages, but don't take that to mean he doesn't want to go when you go. Keep his mind active by taking him with you when you can, instead of leaving him to sleep the day away.

As dogs age, their ability to regulate their body temperature diminishes. Be especially careful that your old guy doesn't get too hot or too cold. There is also the possibility that he may become slightly incontinent. Make sure to rule out a medical cause, and don't chastise him for such accidents. His housetraining hasn't necessarily gone; he's just lost full control. Take him out more often and use a waterproof cover on his bed.

Feeding

As your Siberian ages and his physical activity lessens, he will need fewer calories to maintain a healthy weight. You definitely do not want your older Siberian to be fat. Excess weight puts undue stress on his joints and organ systems. Still, as he gets older and older, he will probably start to lose weight. At that point, you will need to feed your old guy several small meals a day to keep weight on him.

Unless a medical condition exists, older Siberians have no special dietary requirements other than high-quality protein, but keep a close eye on your senior Siberian's teeth. Sore gums can make eating uncomfortable. Some very old Siberians become picky eaters, even without sore gums, so toss your feeding rules out the window and give your old man whatever he will eat.

Grooming

You may find that, as your Siberian gets older, he needs a little more grooming. Grooming can be energizing and an interesting diversion for your dog, as well as an opportunity for you to provide him with the physical contact that contributes to his sense of well-being and fosters good health.

Check your old guy over regularly for lumps and bumps, and have abnormalities seen immediately. Fatty-acid supplements may help as your senior citizen's skin becomes dry, thinner, and more easily injured. And because of the tendency for mature skin and coat to become dry, always use a very mild shampoo and warm water to bathe your older dog. It's common for older dogs to develop calluses on their elbows, because they lie down

more often. Moisturize the calluses and try to prevent them by providing padded mats and dog beds for your senior citizen. Less activity also means fewer opportunities for your Siberian's nails to be worn down, so you'll have to trim them more often. Be extra careful and use very sharp clippers, as his nails may become brittle as he ages.

If your Siberian develops a body odor, find out why. Ear and tooth infections are common sources, as is organ system malfunction. Kidney disease and thyroid problems, both of which can cause odor, are not uncommon in older dogs. A diminishing interest in chewing is also normal in aging dogs, but if yours stops chewing suddenly or looks like he's chewing gingerly, it may be a sign of dental problems. Siberians who have not received proper dental care can develop significant dental disease as they age. Your dog may not enjoy it, but to prevent potentially life-threatening complications from dental disease, he needs his teeth brushed regularly, dental checkups routinely, and professional cleaning as necessary.

Senior Changes

Dogs seem to age much more gracefully than people. Just like people, older dogs may experience cognitive or sensory loss. Unlike people, though, most dogs tend to adapt and carry on just fine, especially with a little help from their people.

Hearing Loss

Some Siberians experience gradual hearing loss as they age, but you probably won't notice anything until the loss is so severe that he repeatedly fails to obey you or startles when you touch him. Hearing loss can't easily be reversed, but your Siberian can adapt with simple changes to his environment. Lower the pitch of your voice and increase the volume. He can still feel vibrations, so stomp on the floor or clap your hands to get his attention. Always make sure he's looking at you when you're trying to communicate, and consider teaching him hand signals. Flashing the yard light or a flashlight is another easy way to get his attention in the dark.

Vision Loss

It is exceedingly rare for Siberian Huskies, even in very old age, to develop nuclear, or lenticular, sclerosis, that bluish or gray haze seen in the pupil of the eye that is caused by the aging of the lens. Old age, or senile, cataracts occur much less frequently in dogs than in humans, and are also rare in Siberians. However, some medical conditions commonly seen in older dogs can cause vision loss. Any sudden changes in vision or appearance of the eyes could signal an emergency, so contact your veterinarian as soon as possible. If your Siberian does begin to lose his vision, you can help him adapt by chattering to him a lot and taking him out to the park or pet store to socialize. Blind dogs do very well at home if you block off hazards such

as stairs and don't move the furniture and other household items around. Using their other senses, blind dogs quickly learn to "map" routes in the yard when they go out so they can find their way back to the door.

Arthritis

Although arthritis isn't inevitable in aging dogs, it is more common in Siberians who have injured a joint or are overweight—another good reason to keep your old guy fit and trim in his senior years.

If your Siberian is very stiff when he stands up, limps when he first starts to walk, avoids steps, and hesitates to jump into the car, ask your veterinarian to check for arthritis. There are medications that help improve joint function. Additionally, you may want to try acupuncture, as Siberians tend to be very responsive to this treatment. Acupuncture increases circulation to the muscles and joint capsule, relieves painful muscle spasms, stimulates nerves and muscles, and releases endorphins to make the dog feel better. When acupuncture is used in conjunction with traditional Chinese herbal medicine, the results may be dramatic.

Cognitive Dysfunction

In rare instances, an older Siberian may suffer from cognitive dysfunction syndrome. CDS is caused by physical and chemical changes that affect the brain function in older dogs. Typically, dogs with this condition wander or pace aimlessly, do not recognize family members, and appear to forget what they are doing while they are doing it. However, there is no test for CDS,

---

BE PREPARED! Cognitive Dysfunction Syndrome

Researchers believe cognitive dysfunction syndrome (CDS) is caused by physical and chemical changes, similar to Alzheimer's disease, that affect brain function. Dogs with CDS may show signs of confusion and various other behavioral changes that are not a normal part of aging. Observe your older Siberian closely using this checklist, document in detail what you see, and consult your veterinarian.

Disorientation/Confusion
☐ Appears lost or confused in the house or yard
☐ Fails to recognize familiar people
☐ Fails to respond to verbal cues or name
☐ Has difficulty finding the door or stands on the hinge side of the door
☐ Appears to forget the reason for going outside

Interaction with family members
☐ Seeks attention less often
☐ Walks away when being petted/cringes when touched
☐ Shows less enthusiasm upon greeting you
☐ No longer greets family members

Sleep and activity changes
☐ Sleeps more during the day
☐ Sleeps less during the night
☐ Wanders or paces more

Loss of housetraining
☐ Urinates indoors
☐ Has accidents indoors soon after being outside
☐ Forgets to ask you to go outside

and there are many other diseases that can cause similar signs (hypothyroidism, diabetes, brain tumors), so it is important to first rule out other medical reasons for the behavior. The good news is that there are effective treatments for CDS.

Senior Health

Never assume that a change in behavior or habits is simply caused by old age; it may be caused by a treatable condition. And because older dogs tend to have more medical problems, you should have some extra tests done during your old guy's annual physical, so you can catch old age problems early and perhaps slow their progress. A urinalysis will test for kidney malfunction, bladder infections, and other problems of the urinary system; a serum chemistry panel provides information about liver, kidney, pancreas, and other organ functions.

Your older Siberian's immune system won't function as effectively, so you'll need to be careful about where he goes and what he's exposed to. He may catch infectious diseases more easily, and the infections could be more severe. Having said that, though, if your Siberian has been traveling with you all his life, he should continue to go, even into very old age—except on airplanes. He'll be better off left at home than in the cargo hold of a plane. And because your older Siberian's immune system isn't as effective anymore, many veterinarians think that dogs over 10 or 12 years of age should not be vaccinated because their immune system can be compromised and because, by the time they're 10 or 12, they have received adequate protection. Note that all vaccines carry a warning that they are to be administered only to healthy animals, so if your older dog is sick, don't vaccinate him.

As dogs age, food may move through the digestive tract more slowly, resulting in constipation. Inactivity and dehydration can also be a contributing factor in this malady. Soaking your Siberian's kibble in water or feeding canned food, and encouraging drinking, might do the trick. However, constipation, vomiting, and diarrhea can also signal some serious disease conditions. When your dog was young, you might have treated all three at home for a few days before seeking help. Now that he's older, and you know that vomiting and diarrhea can dehydrate and weaken an elderly dog rapidly, you won't wait to see the veterinarian.

Although it is not common in the breed, the risk of your Siberian developing bloat (gastric dilatation with or without gastric torsion) increases dramatically with age. Dogs older than seven are at least twice as likely to bloat as are dogs four and under. The classic signs of gastric torsion are restlessness and pacing, salivation, retching, unproductive attempts to vomit, increased heart rate, and enlargement of the abdomen. Thumping the abdomen produces a hollow sound. Bloat is life threatening, and emergency treatment must be obtained immediately. Do not wait for signs to progress before seeking veterinary care. Does your Siberian gulp his food? Research suggests that forcing him to eat more slowly may help reduce the risk. You can accomplish this with a wide, shallow food bowl and a large, clean rock. Put the rock in the middle of the bowl and pour the food around it. Eating around the rock is a slower process. Feeding your older Siberian two meals a day and keeping him as quiet as possible before and after eating may also lower his risk for bloat.

Thirty years ago, most dogs died before they were old enough to develop cancer. Better food, better veterinary care, and the easy life have given Siberian owners more happy years with their dogs, but with that longer life comes an increased risk of cancer. As your Siberian ages, his risk of developing mast cell tumors, lymphoma, and cancers of the spleen and liver increases. Some of the major symptoms of cancer are lumps or bumps that persist or grow, sores that don't heal, weight loss, loss of appetite, offensive odor, difficulty eating or swallowing, loss of stamina, and difficulty in breathing, urinating, or defecating. Use your Routine Health Checklist (page 96) to record any changes and take the findings to your veterinarian immediately. Although some cancers have a better prognosis than others, effective cancer treatment options for dogs have increased and new protocols are constantly being developed. Chemotherapy, radiation, surgery, and antiangiogenic and photodynamic therapies are commonly used alone or in combination, depending on the type of cancer being treated and its location in the body. You should know that, unlike people, dogs tolerate chemotherapy quite well, so their quality of life during treatment is usually good.

Chapter Ten

The Siberian Husky Standard

A breed standard "portrays what, in the minds of its compilers, would be the ideal dog of the breed. Ideal in type, in structure, in gait, in temperament—the ideal in every aspect," says the AKC's *Complete Dog Book*. The compilers of a breed standard are, in all cases, members of that breed's parent club, in this case, the Siberian Husky Club of America. AKC-approved dog show judges compare each dog they judge with the ideal as described in the standard. Everything in the Siberian Husky standard, with the exception of a few aesthetically pleasing inclusions added between 1930 and 1990, points the way to the demand for proper Siberian structure, which ordains correct Siberian movement. This is as it should be, since the dog's job is to move down the trail efficiently.

The Standard Defined

The first paragraph of any breed standard describes the overall appearance of the dog, with the details, such as eye shape and leg length, coming later. The General Appearance paragraph of the current Siberian Husky breed standard says, "The Siberian Husky is a medium-sized working dog, quick and light on his feet and graceful in action. His moderately compact and well furred body, erect ears and brush tail suggest his Northern heritage. His characteristic gait is smooth and seemingly effortless. He performs his original function in harness most capably, carrying a light load at a moderate speed over great distances. His body proportions and form reflect this basic balance of power, speed and endurance."

Head
1. **Head:** Medium size, in proportion to body; slightly rounded on top, tapering from the widest point of the eyes; stop well-defined, bridge of the nose is straight from stop to tip.
2. **Eyes:** Almond shaped, moderately spaced, set a trifle obliquely. Eyes brown or blue in color; one of each or parti-colored acceptable.

3. **Ears:** Medium size, triangular in shape, close fitting, set high on the head. Thick, well furred, strongly erect, slightly rounded tips pointing straight up.
4. **Muzzle:** Medium length (distance from tip of nose to stop is equal to distance from stop to occiput); medium width, tapering gradually to the nose, tip neither pointed nor square. Lips well pigmented, close fitting.
5. **Nose:** Black in gray, brown, and black dogs; liver in copper dogs; may be flesh-colored in pure white dogs. Pink-streaked "snow nose" is acceptable.
6. **Teeth:** Closing in a scissors bite.

Body

1. **Neck:** Medium length, arched, carried erect when standing, extended when moving.
2. **Back:** Medium length, strong, level topline.
3. **Loin:** Taut, lean, narrower than rib cage, with a slight tuck-up.
4. **Chest:** Deep and strong, not too broad, with deepest point just behind and level with the elbows; ribs well sprung from spine but flattened on sides to allow for freedom of action.
5. **Shoulders:** Powerful, well laid back; upper arm angles slightly backward from point of shoulder to elbow, is never perpendicular to the ground. Muscles and ligaments holding shoulder to rib cage are firm and well-developed.

FYI: Siberian Movement

In the show ring at a moderately fast (for a human) trot, or on the trail trotting at 12–14 miles per hour (19–22 kph), the Siberian should be the picture of efficiency—smooth and seemingly effortless ground-eating forward motion. To trot at a moderate speed for long distances without tiring, the Siberian's energy cannot be wasted on movements that do not contribute to forward motion. Bouncing or prancing up and down, or rolling from side to side is wasted motion.

- The front foot should reach forward to touch the ground under the dog's nose.
- The rear foot should land under the middle of the dog's body, then push off to propel him forward.
- As his speed increases, his legs gradually angle inward until the pads are falling on a line directly under the longitudinal center of the body, and the imprints of the hind feet tend to cover the tracks left by the front.
- His feet should lift off the ground just enough to clear the ground, so you won't see footpads coming at you but you will see footpads going away.
- His forelegs and hind legs should be carried straight forward, with neither elbows nor stifles turning in or out.
- His topline should remain firm and steady, without bouncing or rolling.
- His head and neck should be extended forward almost level with the topline.
- The tail should be trailing horizontally in line with his topline.

Many, many dogs with less than perfect movement make it to Nome every year, and your Siberian won't need to perfectly display these qualities to go biking with you. Still, it's always interesting to see just how closely your dog fits the standard.

6. **Forelegs:** Moderately spaced, parallel, straight, elbows turn neither in nor out; pasterns slightly slanted, strong, flexible; length of leg from elbow to ground is slightly more than distance from elbow to withers.
7. **Feet:** Oval but not long, medium sized; compact, well furred between toes and pads; pads tough, thickly cushioned.
8. **Hind legs:** Moderately spaced and parallel; upper thigh well muscled, powerful; stifles well bent; hock joint well defined.
9. **Croup and tail:** Croup slopes away from the spine at 30 degree angle. Well furred tail set on just below the level of the topline.

View from the Front
1. **Skull:** Neither clumsy nor heavy, or too finely chiseled.
2. **Thorax:** Deep chest with prominent sternum.
3. **Rib Cage:** Ribs are flattened on the sides to allow freedom of action.
4. **Elbows:** Close to the body and turned neither in nor out.
5. **Legs and feet:** Moderately spaced, parallel, straight; pasterns (wrists) long; feet oval; toes usually turn out ever so slightly when standing freely.

The Whys and Wherefores of the Standard

"The Siberian Husky is a medium-sized working dog, quick and light on his feet and free and graceful in action . . . . His characteristic gait is smooth and seemingly effortless. He performs his original function in harness most capably, carrying a light load at a moderate speed over great distances. His body proportions and form reflect this basic balance of power, speed and endurance . . . . The Siberian Husky never appears so heavy or coarse as to suggest a freighting animal nor is he so light and fragile as to suggest a sprint-racing animal. In both sexes the Siberian Husky gives the appearance of being capable of great endurance." From the November 28, 1990, AKC Siberian Husky Standard.

The Siberian standard describes the ideal form of a dog who evolved over centuries to survive in an arctic environment while pulling a light load at a moderate speed over long distances. It should be noted that the vast majority of the Siberian's features, from eye shape to rib-cage length, are functional rather than aesthetic and were attained through natural selection rather than human intervention. To be successfully efficient, the dog must have the following characteristics:

- The medium sized, moderately compact, well proportioned and balanced body required to achieve the efficient, floating gait needed to go the distance without tiring.
- A deep, strong, but not broad chest to allow the front legs to swing straight forward and back unimpeded. The rib cage is long to allow room for lung expansion.
- Powerful hindquarters to propel the dog forward.
- Medium-sized, compact, oval feet, with strong toes and tough, thick pads that operate like snowshoes, provide balance and power in turns, and traction on snow and ice.
- A double coat to conserve body heat in winter and insulate from heat in summer.
- Eyes almond shaped and set a trifle obliquely to leave less eyeball exposed to the elements.
- Thick, well-furred, medium-sized, strongly erect and very mobile ears that can be folded shut and pinned back into the ruff to

protect them from blowing snow and frostbite, and focused in almost any direction to better hear his driver or the faint noise of small prey.

- A medium length muzzle, long enough to both preheat and moisturize inhaled cold air and to cool the dog's blood as he works.
- A well-furred tail of fox-brush shape that reaches to his hocks, ensuring he can cover his face with it when curled up to sleep in the snow. The tail is also used as a rudder when running.
- Long sloping pasterns which absorb the shock of each footfall, allowing the dog to go the distance comfortably.

Temperament According to the Standard

Correct temperament is more important than good shoulders, good feet, or correct muzzle length. The AKC Siberian Husky standard states, "The characteristic temperament of the Siberian Husky is friendly and gentle, but also alert and outgoing. He does not display the possessive qualities of the guard dog, nor is he overly suspicious of strangers or aggressive with other dogs. Some measure of reserve and dignity may be expected in the mature dog. His intelligence, tractability, and eager disposition make him an agreeable companion and willing worker."

When you're out on the trail alone in the dark and it's –20°F (–29°C), the last thing you want is an aggressive dog picking fights in the team. Neither do you want a quivering bowl of jelly hiding in the corner of your living room, afraid of his own shadow. The Siberian, as a working sled dog, a family member, or a show dog must be a team dog and is expected to be confident, friendly, and outgoing to people and other dogs.

Breed Truths

Balance and Proportions

In sled dogs, the more efficient the skeleton is, the less energy is required to move the dog down the trail. Good balance is achieved when the four major bones, the scapula, humerus, pelvis, and femur, are of equal length. Poor balance will affect a dog's gait, which will affect performance. For example, a dog with a short pelvis and longer femur will be fast initially, but tire quickly and/or be easily injured. The Siberian standard requires the length of the body from the point of the shoulder to the rear point of the croup to be slightly longer than the height of the body from the ground to the top of the withers. Research shows that the vast majority of good working sled dogs are about 10 percent longer than they are tall. The standard also requires the length of leg from elbow to ground to be slightly more than the distance from the elbow to the top of the withers. Research shows that most good working sled dogs' legs from elbow to ground are about 5 percent longer than from elbow to withers. Dogs who are out of proportion have less endurance.

Resources

Organizations

All Breed
American Kennel Club
www.akc.org

United Kennel Club
www.ukcdogs.com/WebSite.nsf/
WebPages/Home

Canadian Kennel Club
www.ckc.ca

Fédération Cynologique
Internationale
www.fci.be

Siberian Husky
Siberian Husky Club of America
(contains links to area clubs)
www.shca.org/

Siberian Husky Club of Canada
www.siberianhuskyclubofcanada.com

International Siberian Husky Club
www.ishclub.org

Research/Health

AKC Canine Health Foundation
www.akcchf.org

Morris Animal Foundation
www.morrisanimalfoundation.org

Canine Health Information Center
www.caninehealthinfo.org

OFA/CERF
www.offa.org

Working Dog Web Pages

Sled Dog Central
www.sleddogcentral.com

Working Dog Web
www.workingdogweb.com

Index

THE TEAM BEHIND THE *TRAIN YOUR DOG* DVD

Host **Nicole Wilde** is a certified Pet Dog Trainer and internationally recognized author and lecturer. Her books include *So You Want to Be a Dog Trainer* and *Help for Your Fearful Dog* (Phantom Publishing). In addition to working with dogs, Nicole has been working with wolves and wolf hybrids for over fifteen years and is considered an expert in the field.

Host **Laura Bourhenne** is a Professional Member of the Association of Pet Dog Trainers, and holds a degree in Exotic Animal Training. She has trained many species of animals including several species of primates, birds of prey, and many more. Laura is striving to enrich the lives of pets by training and educating the people they live with.

Director **Leo Zahn** is an award winning director/cinematographer/editor of television commercials, movies, and documentaries. He has directed and edited more than a dozen instructional DVDs through the Picture Company, a subsidiary of Picture Palace, Inc., based in Los Angeles.